7/10

W9-BWH-608

NINJAS HAVE ISSUES

GREG STONES

CHRONICLE BOOKS

SAN FRANCISCO

Huge thanks to my parents for buying me a ninja suit when I was eleven, to my wife for tolerating how many hours I spend in my studio, to Steve Mockus for editing each of my books into something that people will actually enjoy, and to Sho Kosugi for being the coolest ninja ever.

Library of Congress Cataloging-in-Publication Data Available.

ISBN 978-1-4521-4474-0

Designed by Michael Morris

10 9 8 7 6 5 4 3 2 1

Chronicle Books LLC
680 Second Street
San Francisco, California 94107
www.chroniclebooks.com

Chronicle Books publishes distinctive books and gifts. From award-winning children's titles, bestselling cookbooks, and eclectic pop culture to acclaimed works of art and design, stationery, andjournals, we craft publishing that's instantly recognizable for its spirit and creativity. Enjoy our publishing and become part of our community at www.chroniclebooks.com.

NINJAS HAVE ISSUES WITH . . .

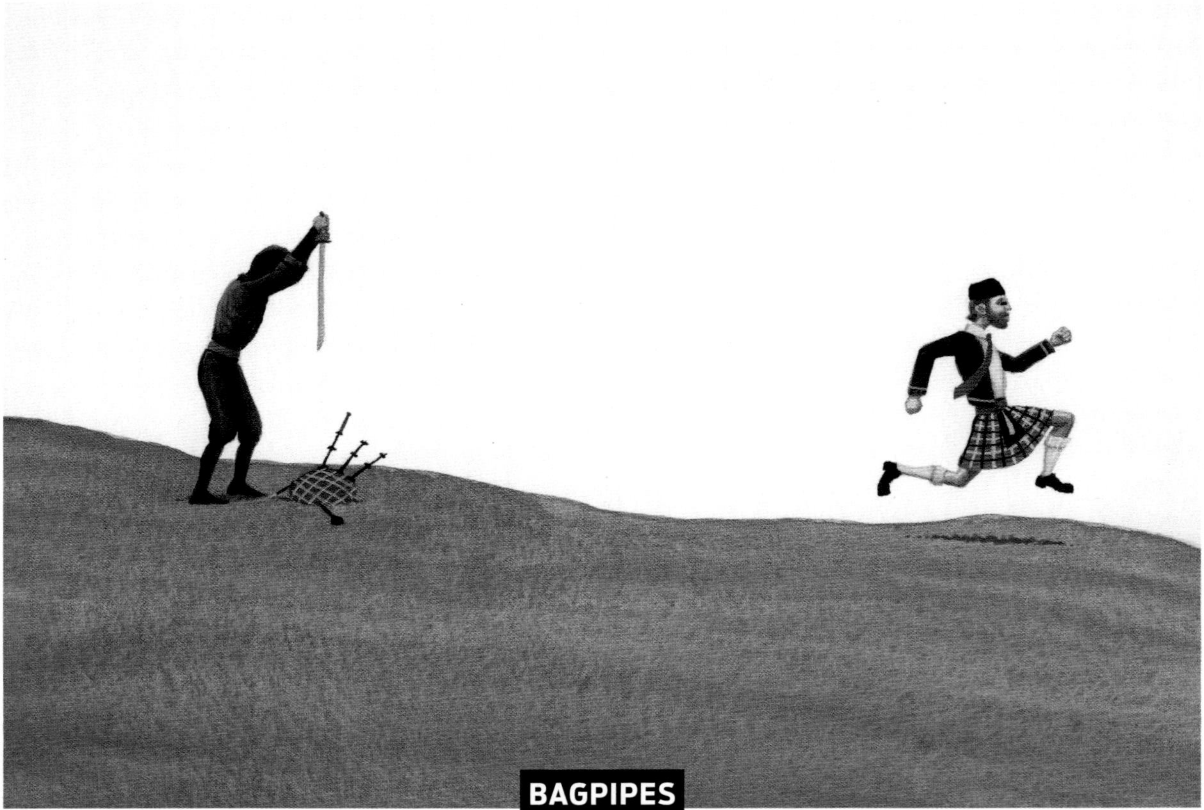

BAGPIPES

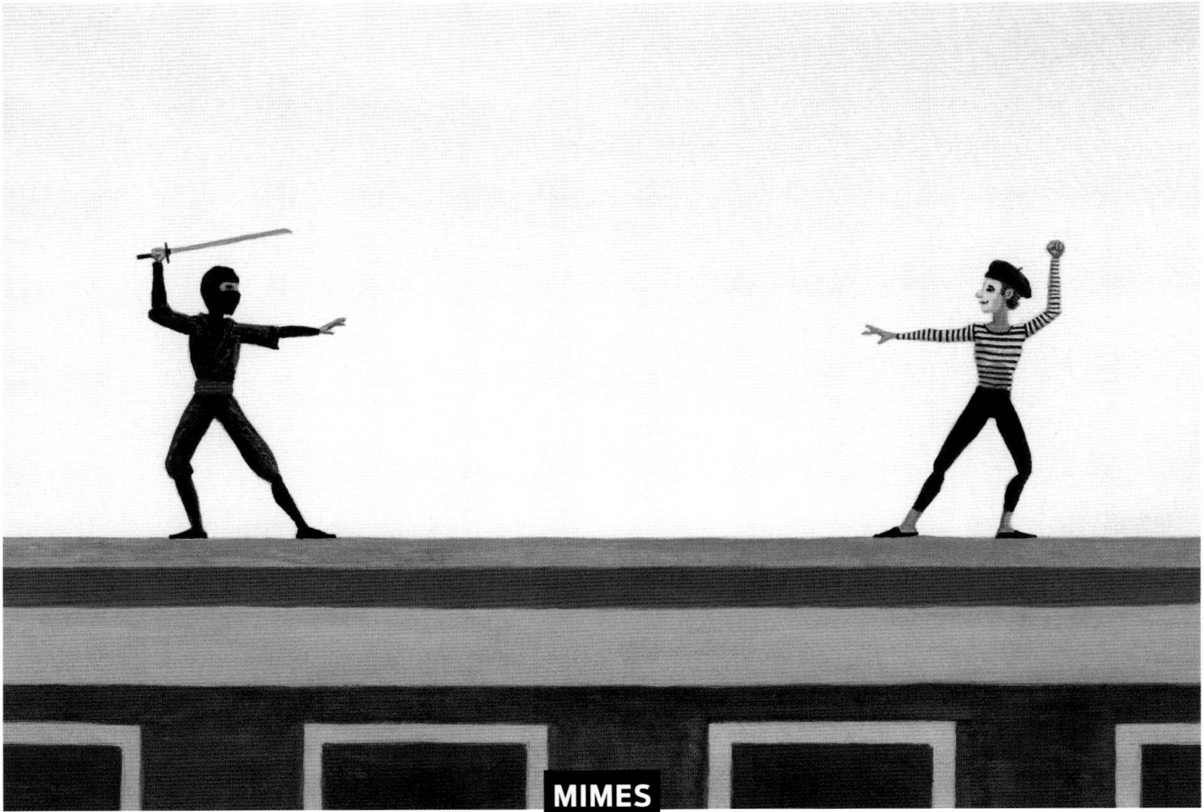

MIMES

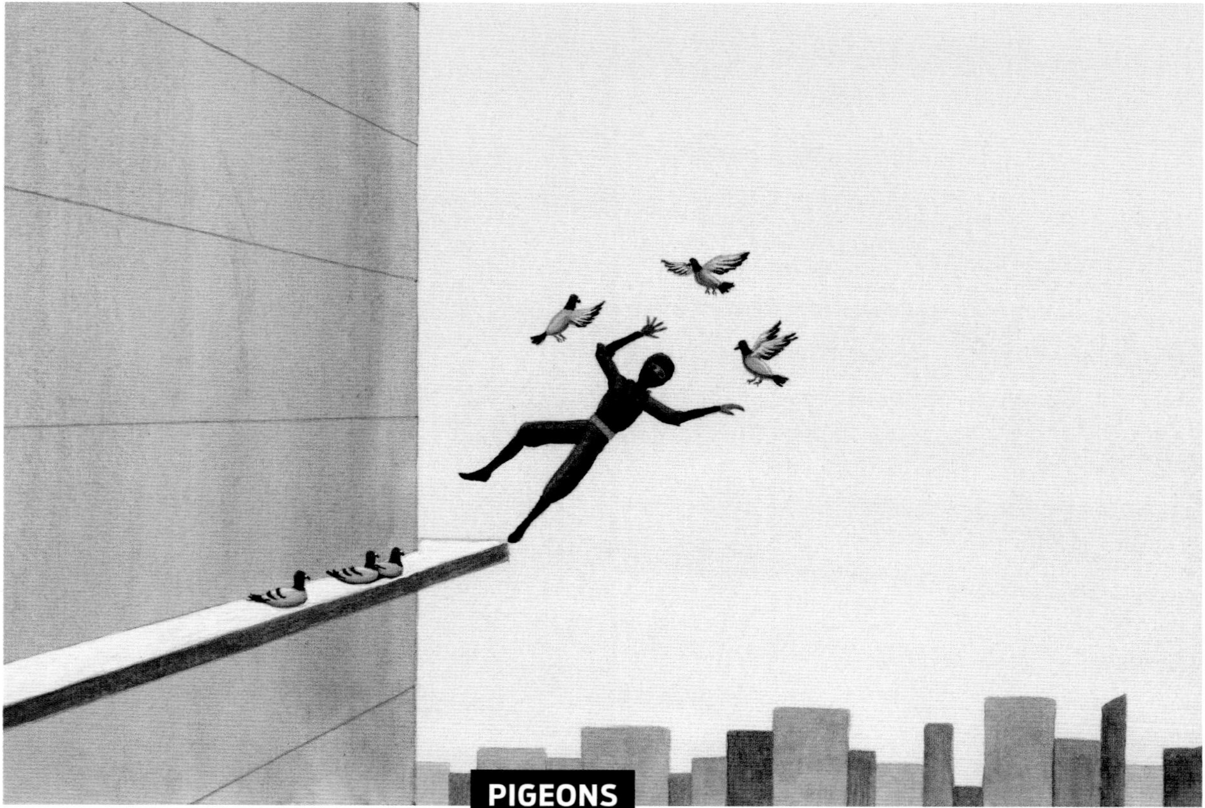

PIGEONS

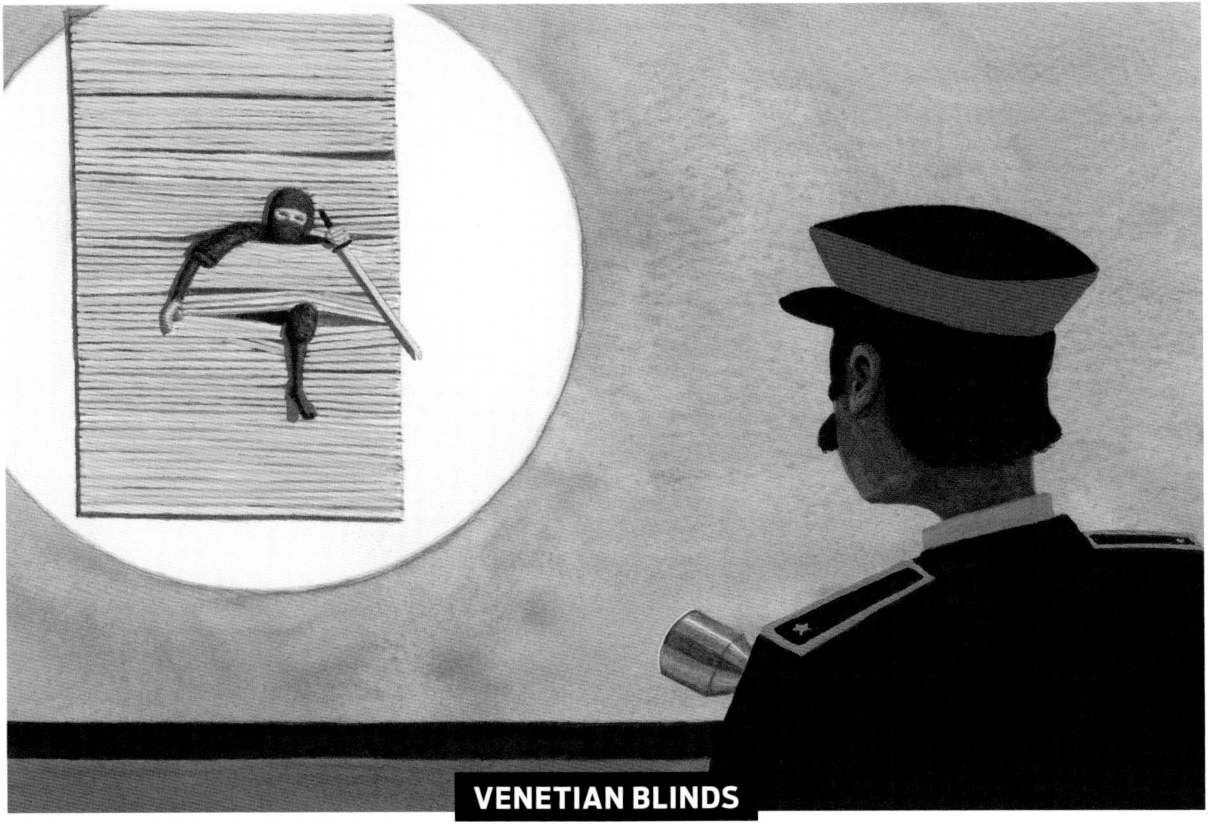

VENETIAN BLINDS

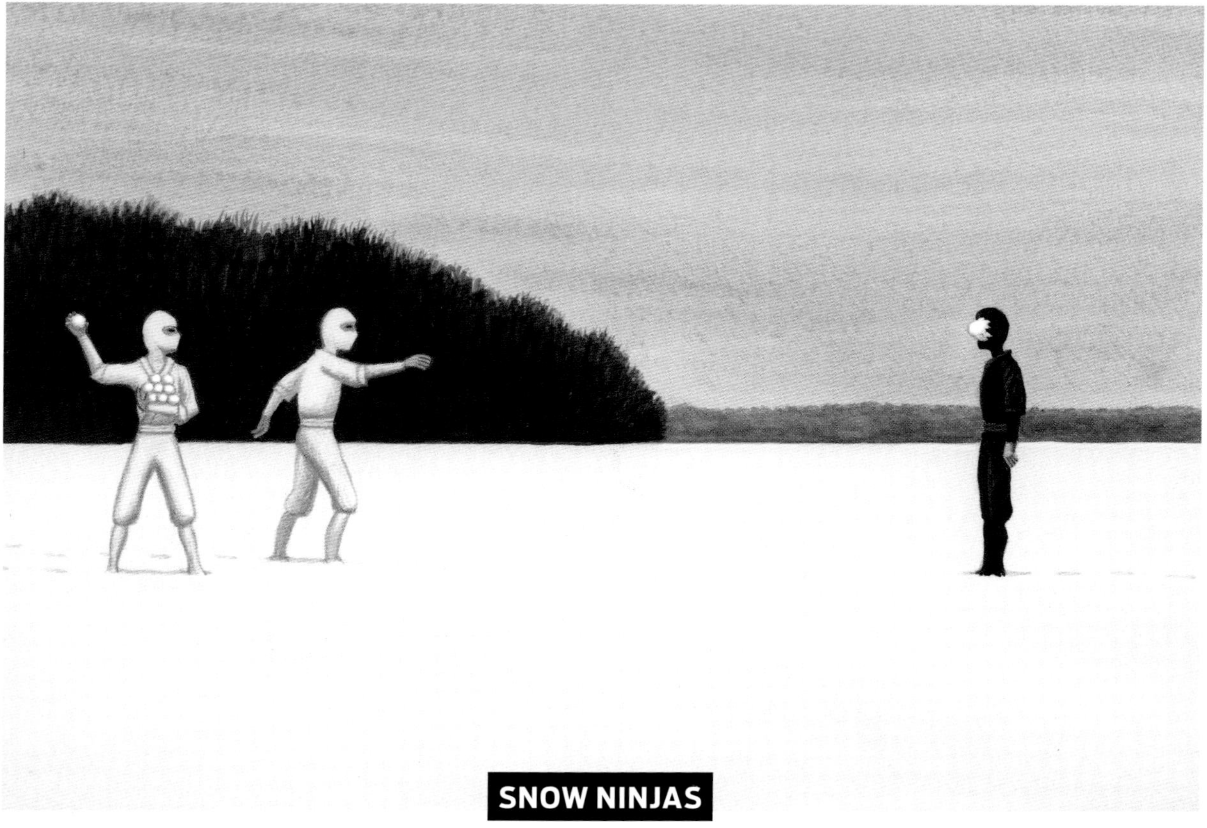

SNOW NINJAS

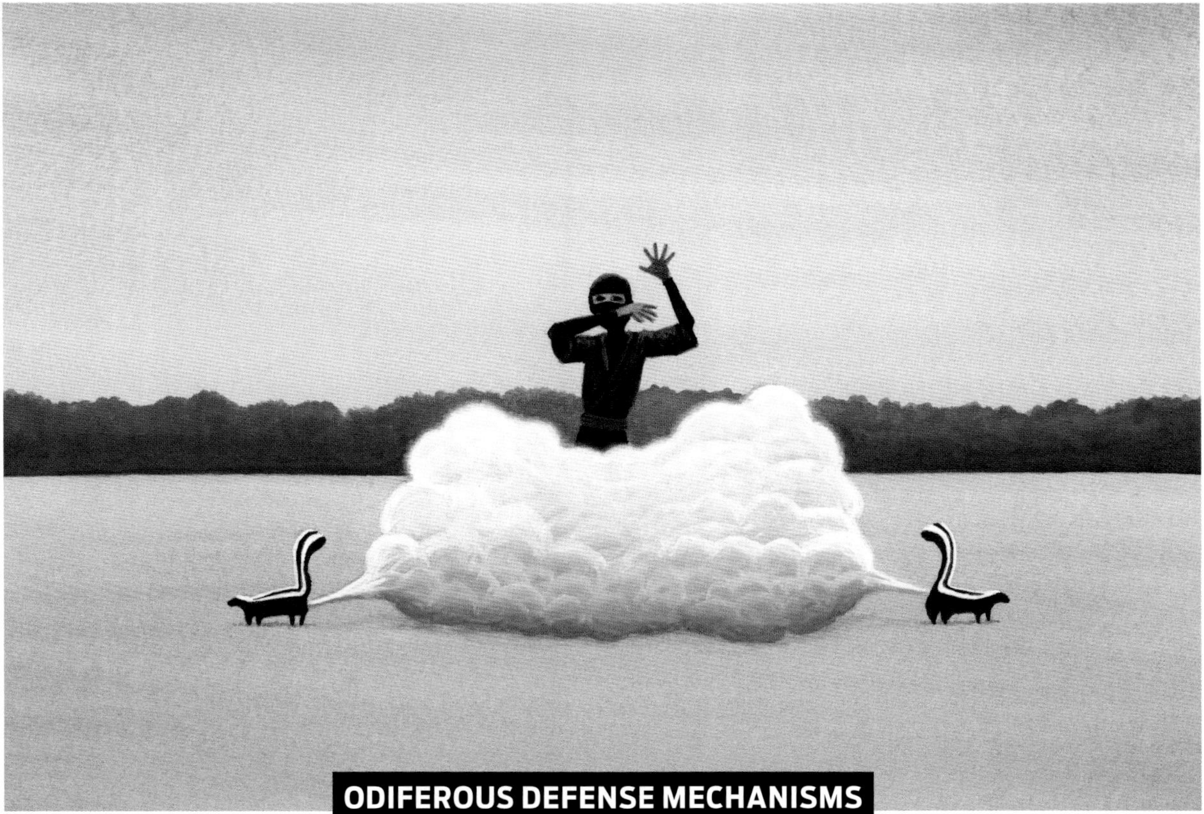

ODIFEROUS DEFENSE MECHANISMS

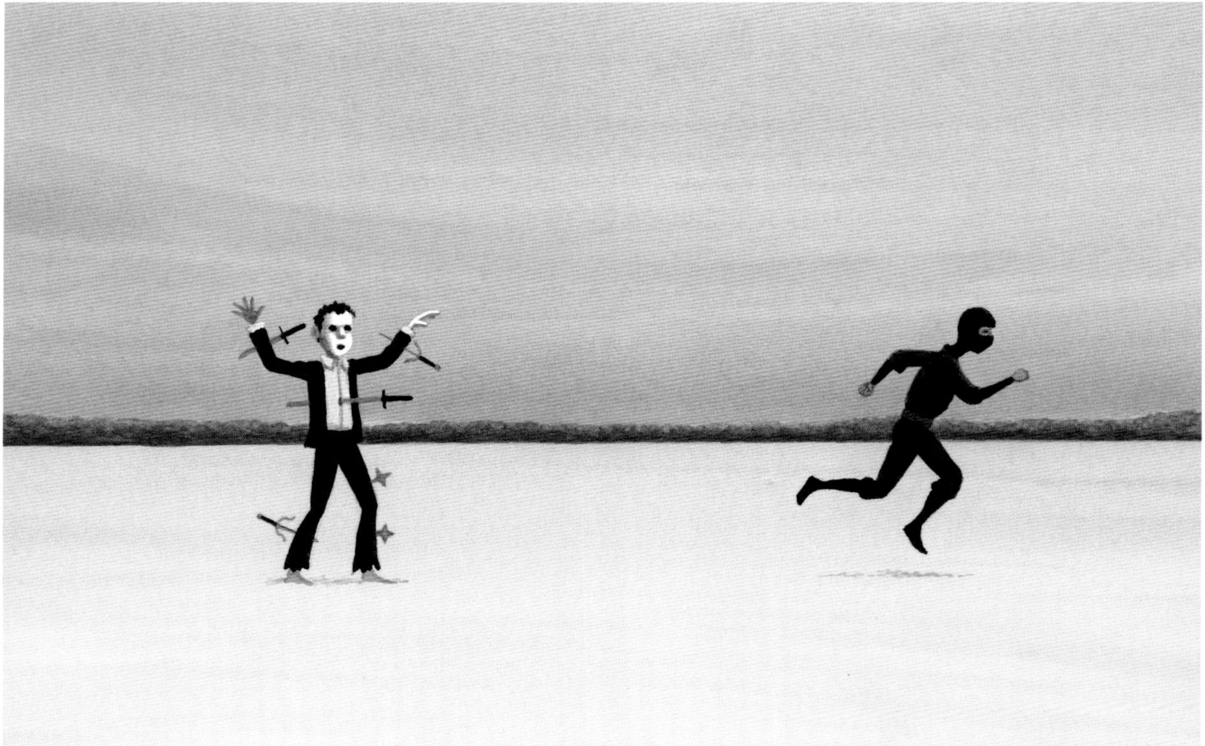

ZOMBIES

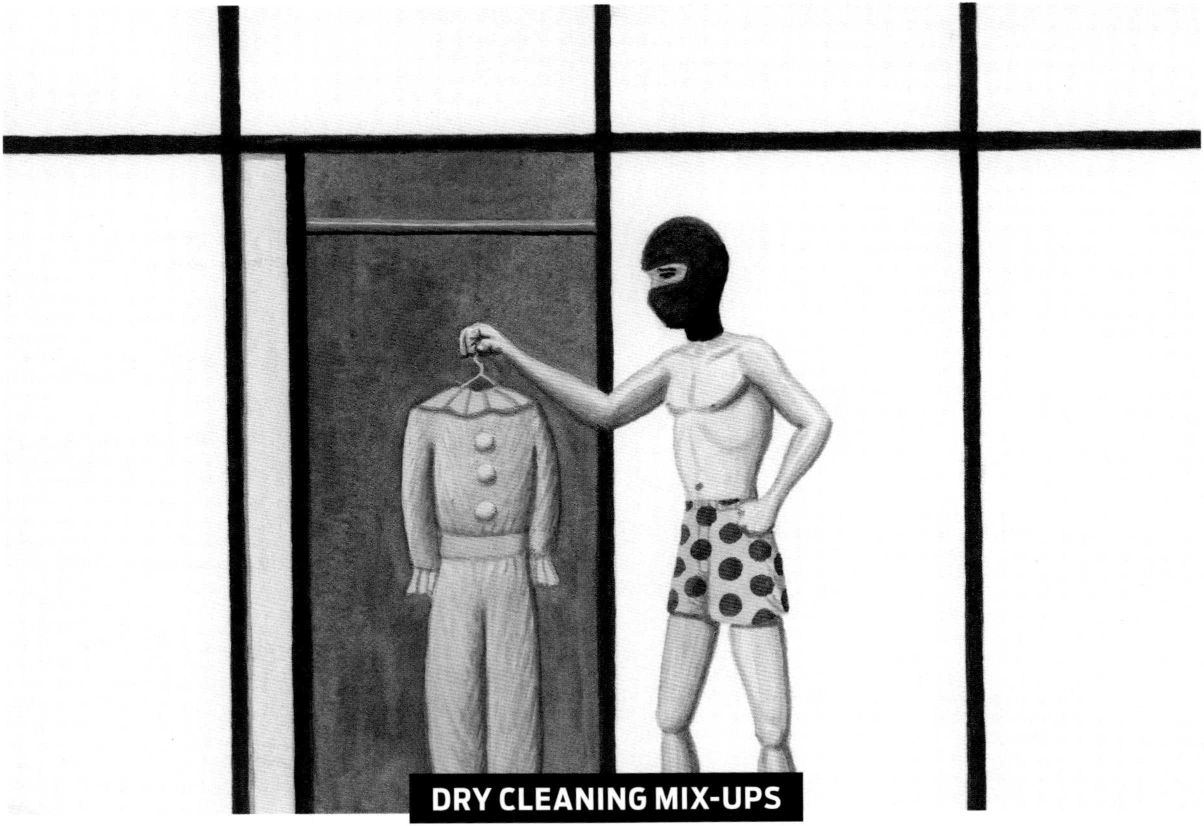

DRY CLEANING MIX-UPS

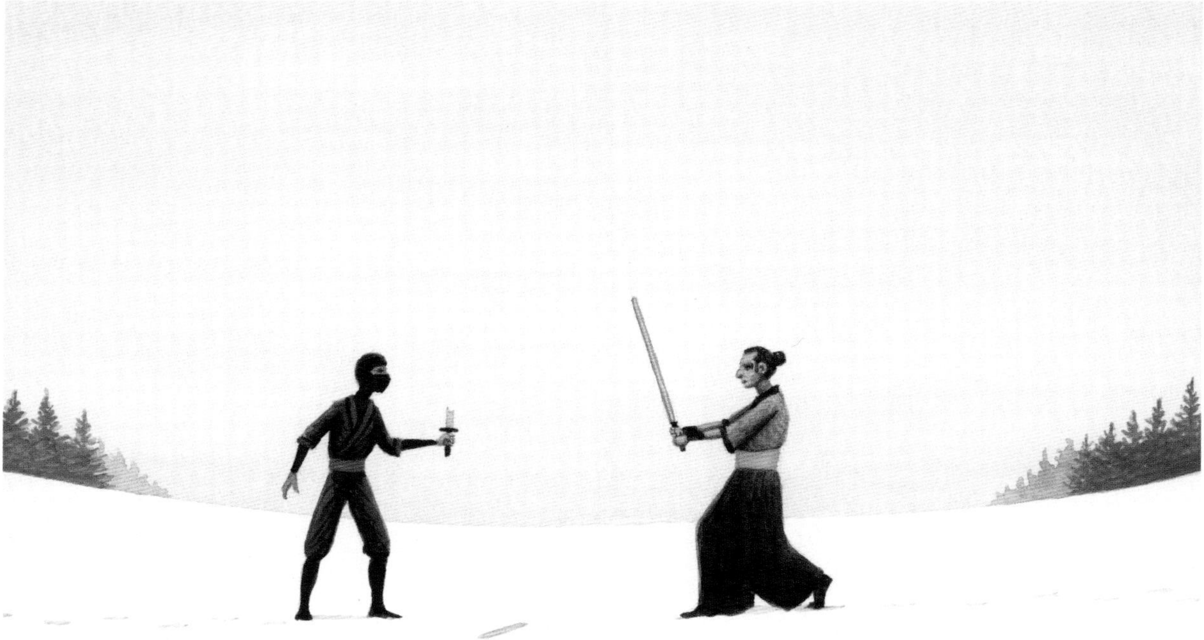

LASER SWORDS

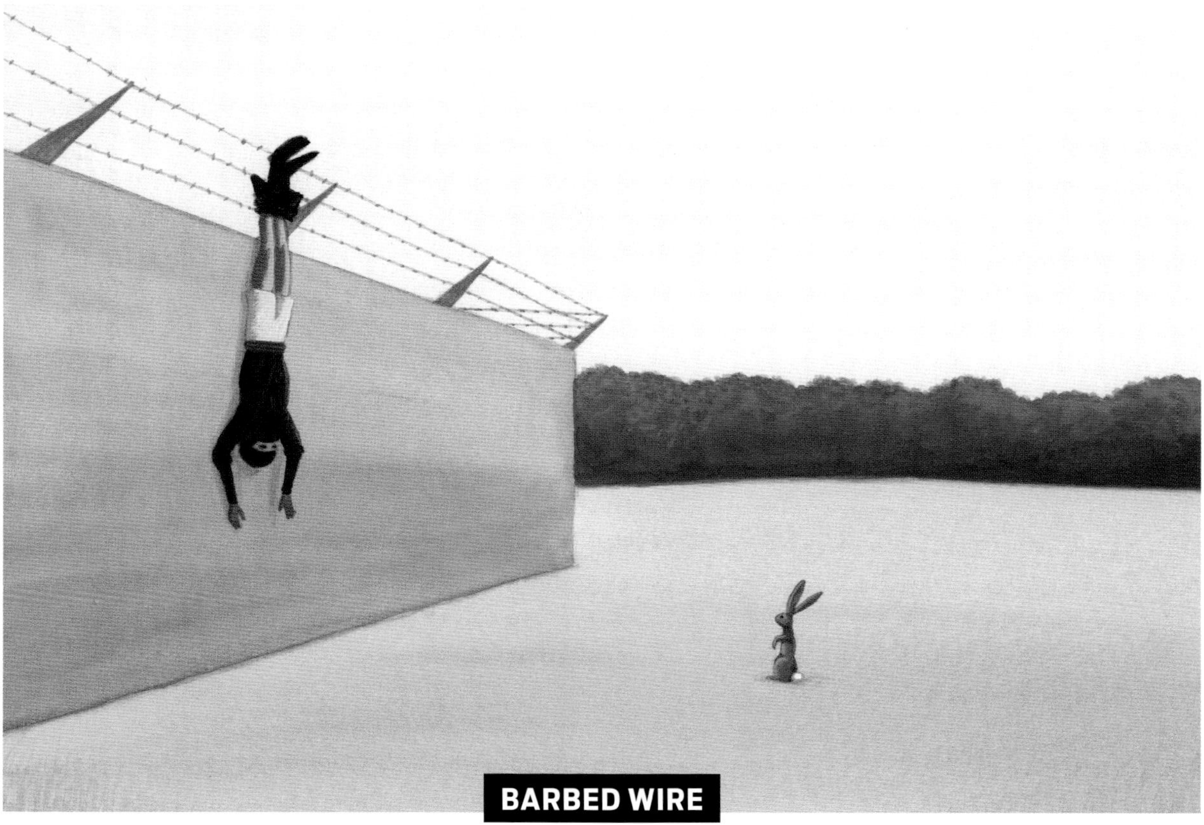

BARBED WIRE

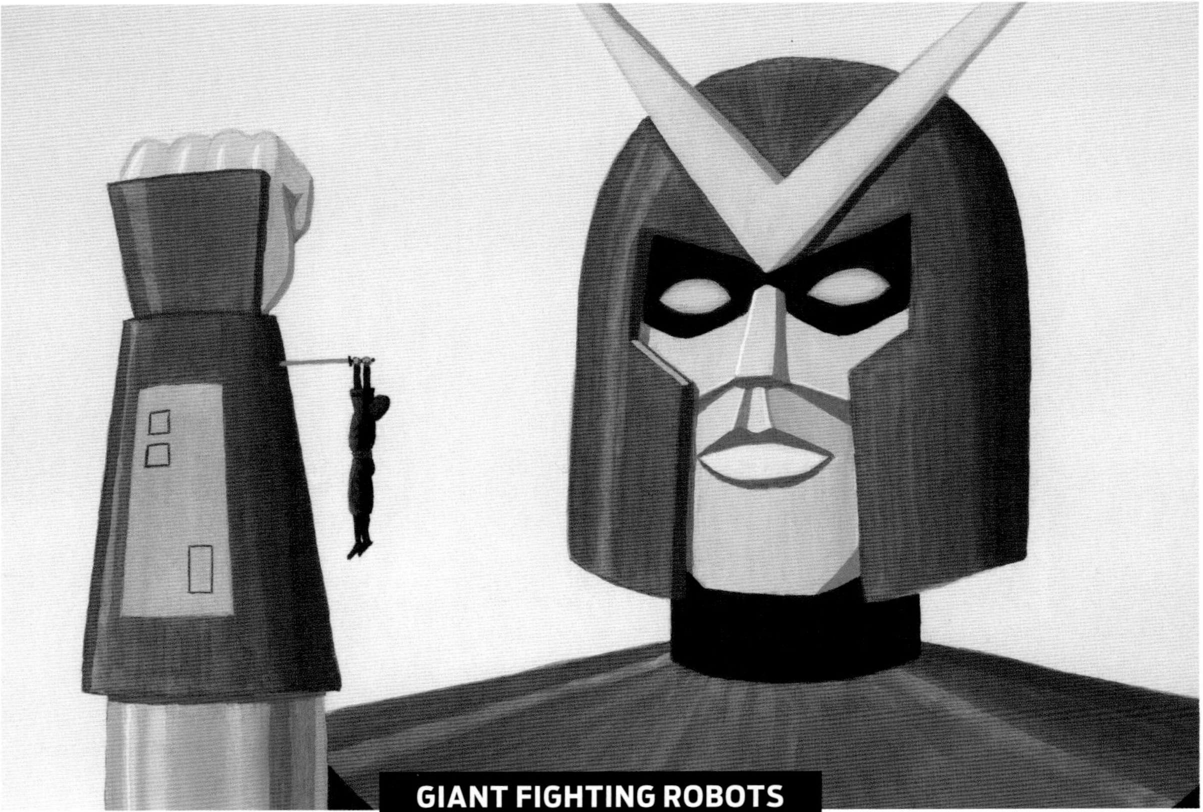

GIANT FIGHTING ROBOTS

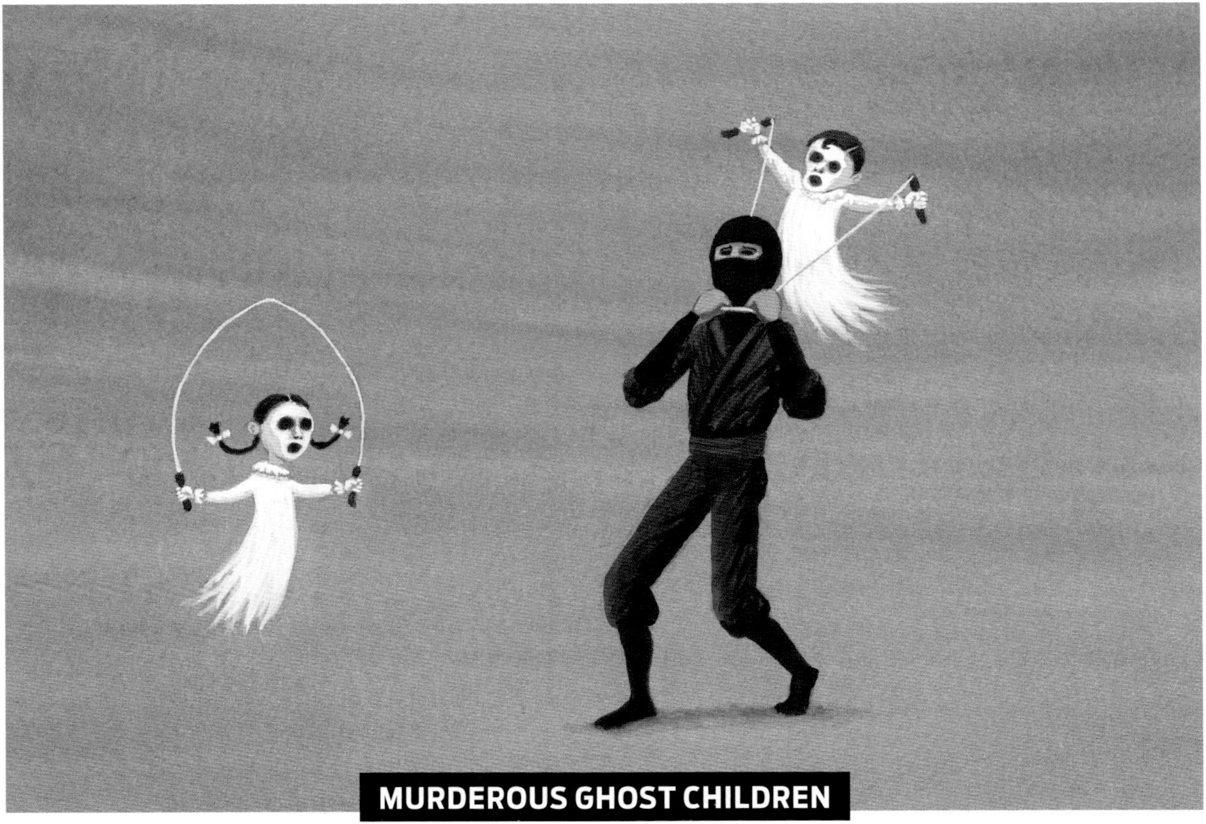

MURDEROUS GHOST CHILDREN

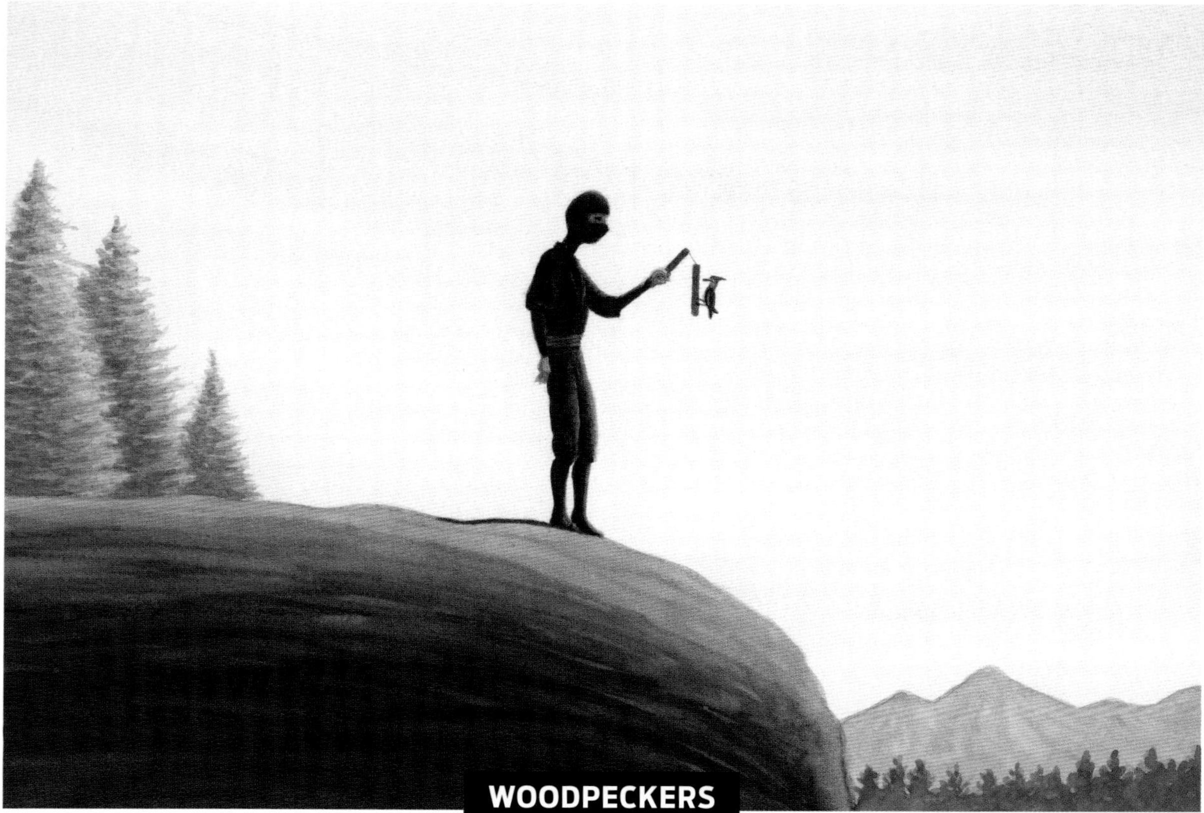

WOODPECKERS

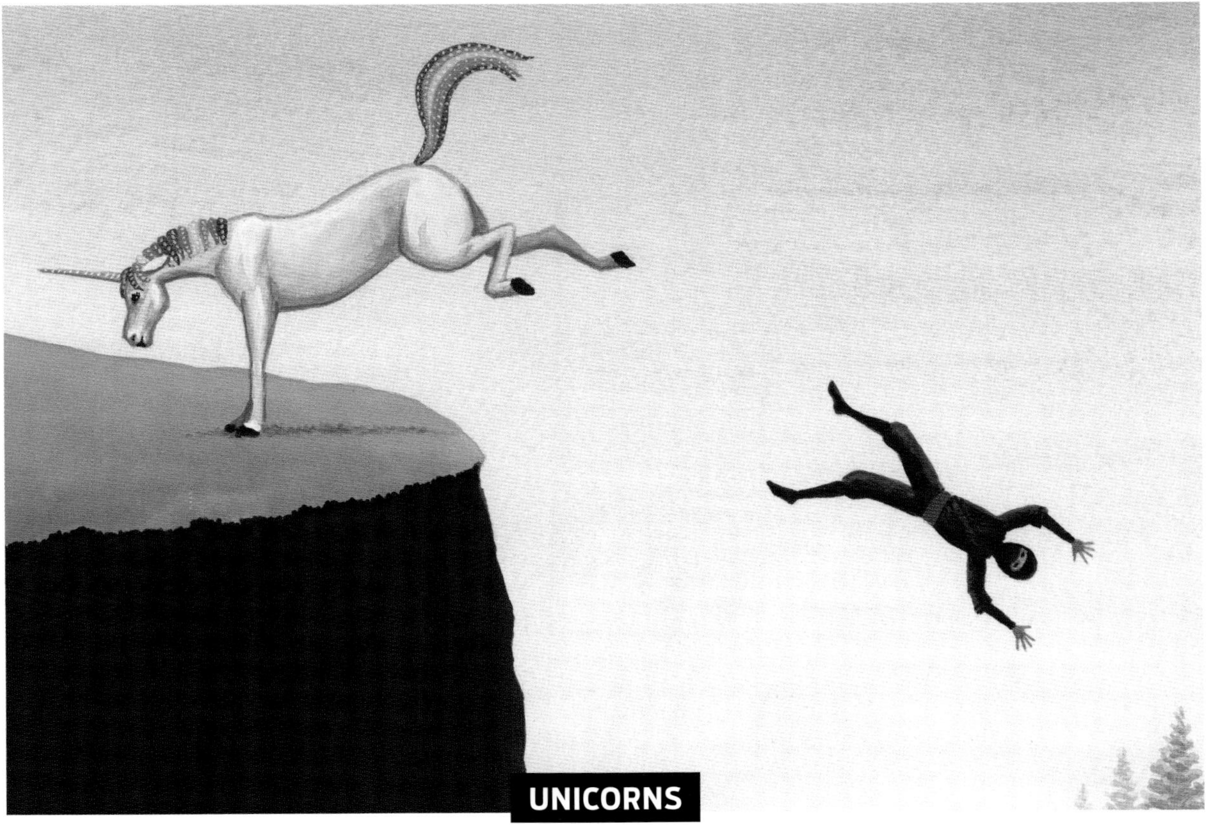

UNICORNS

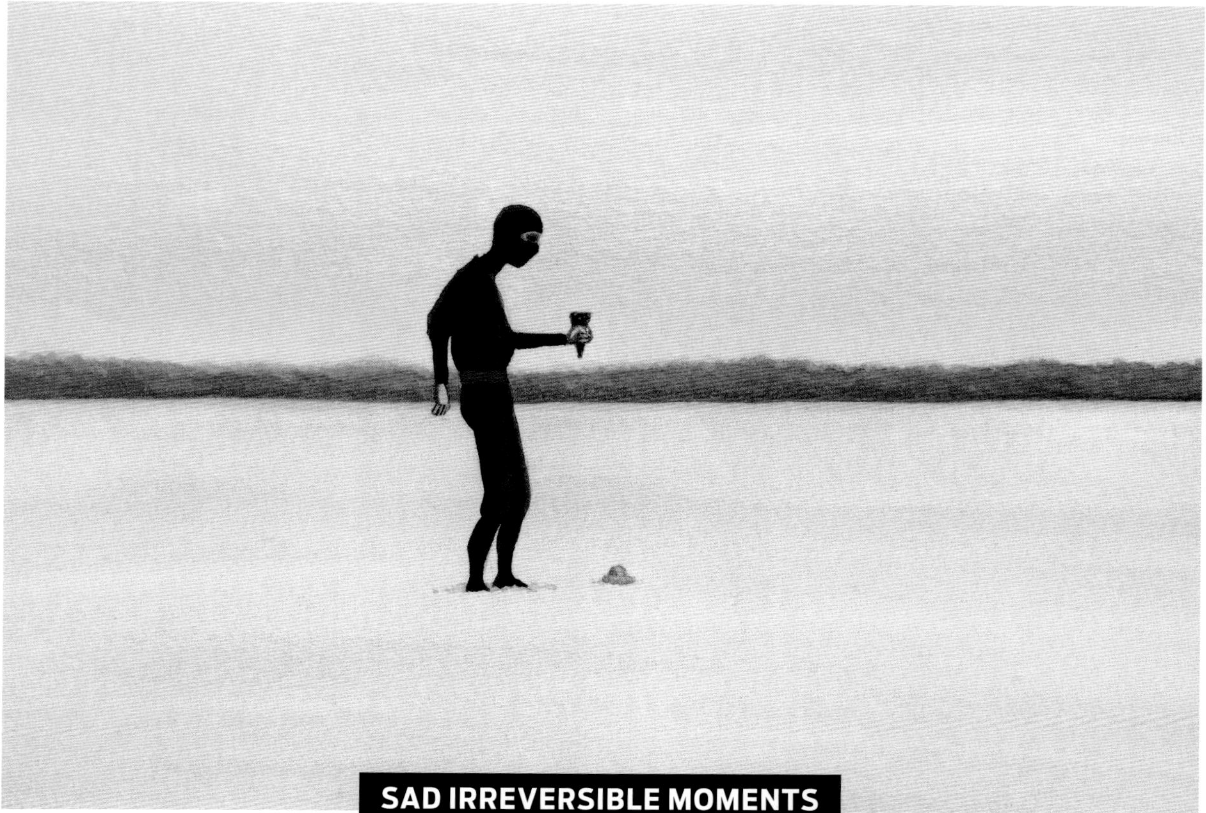

SAD IRREVERSIBLE MOMENTS

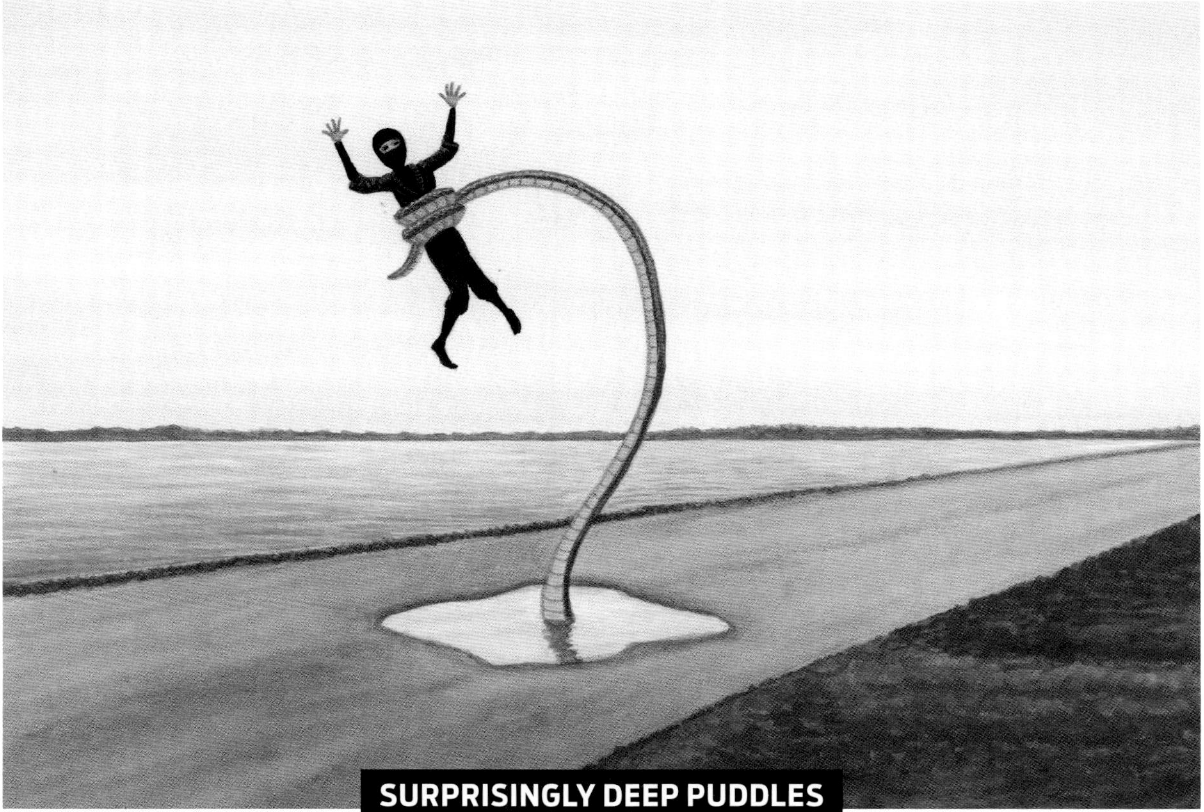

SURPRISINGLY DEEP PUDDLES

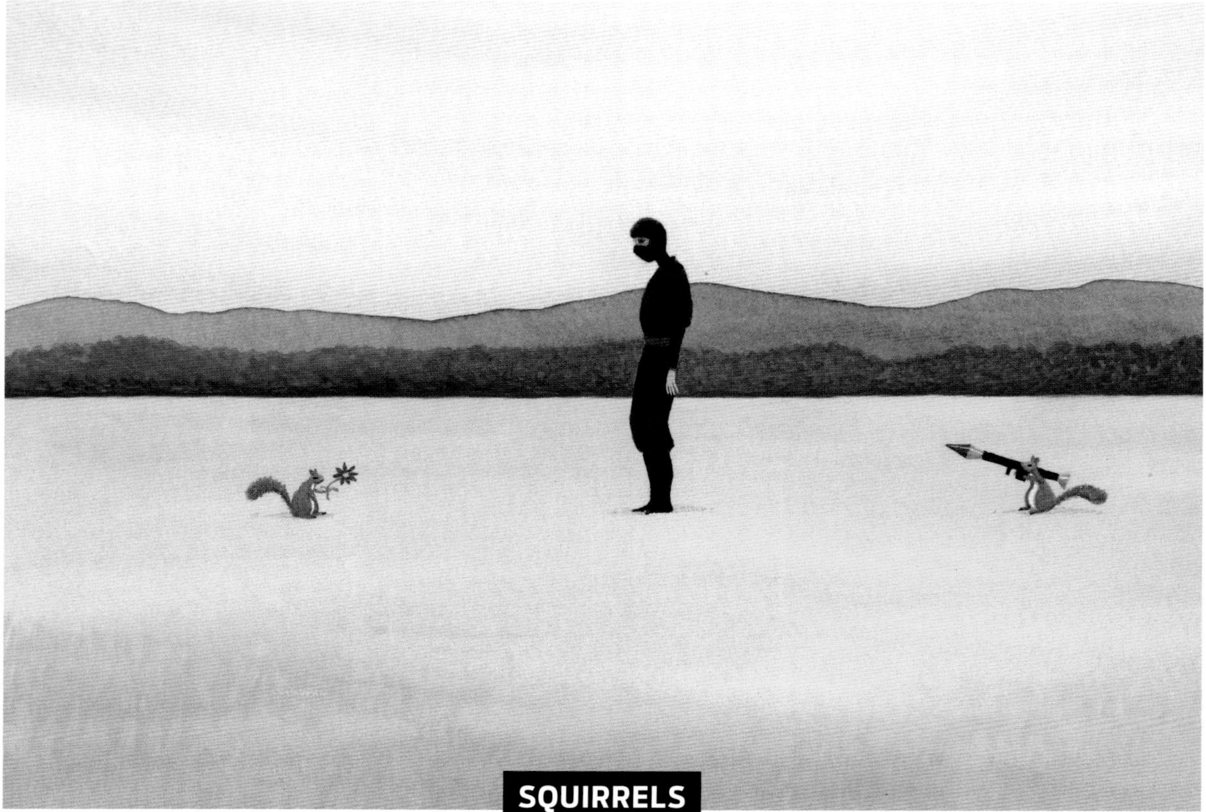

SQUIRRELS

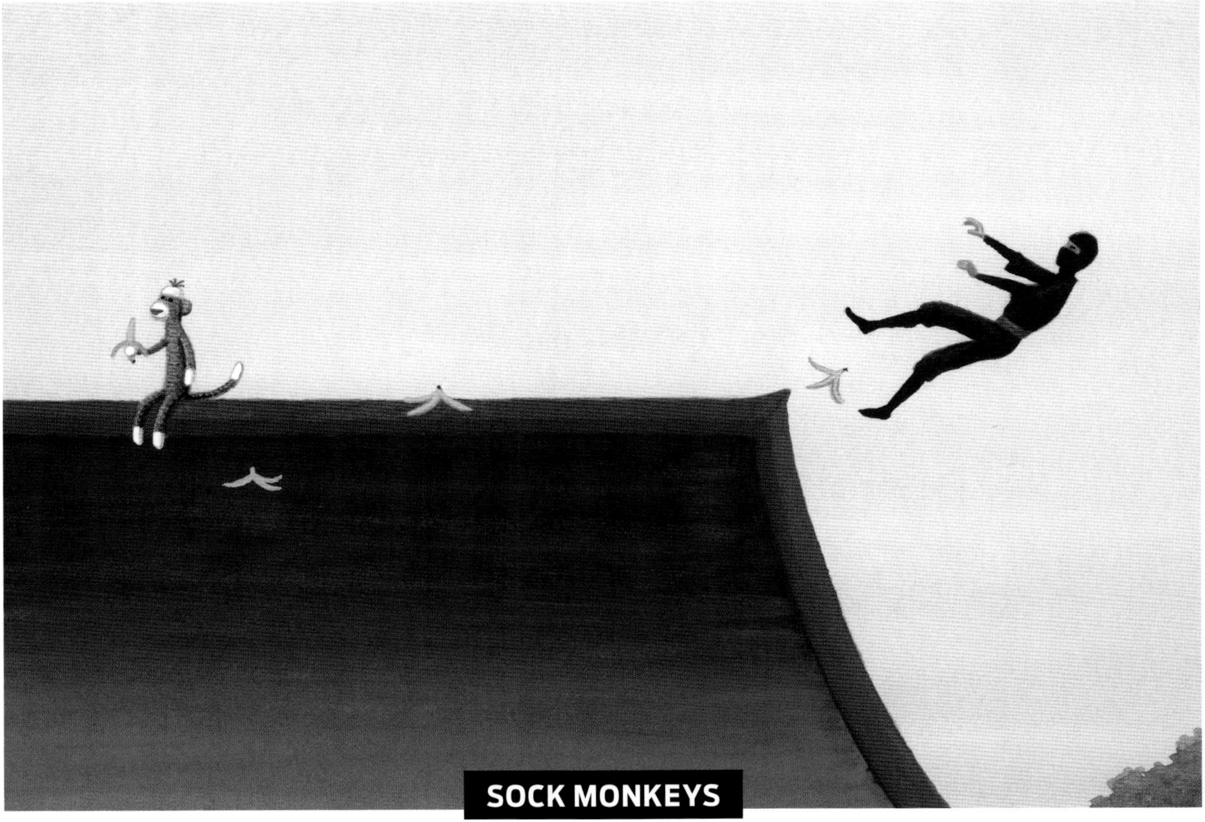
SOCK MONKEYS

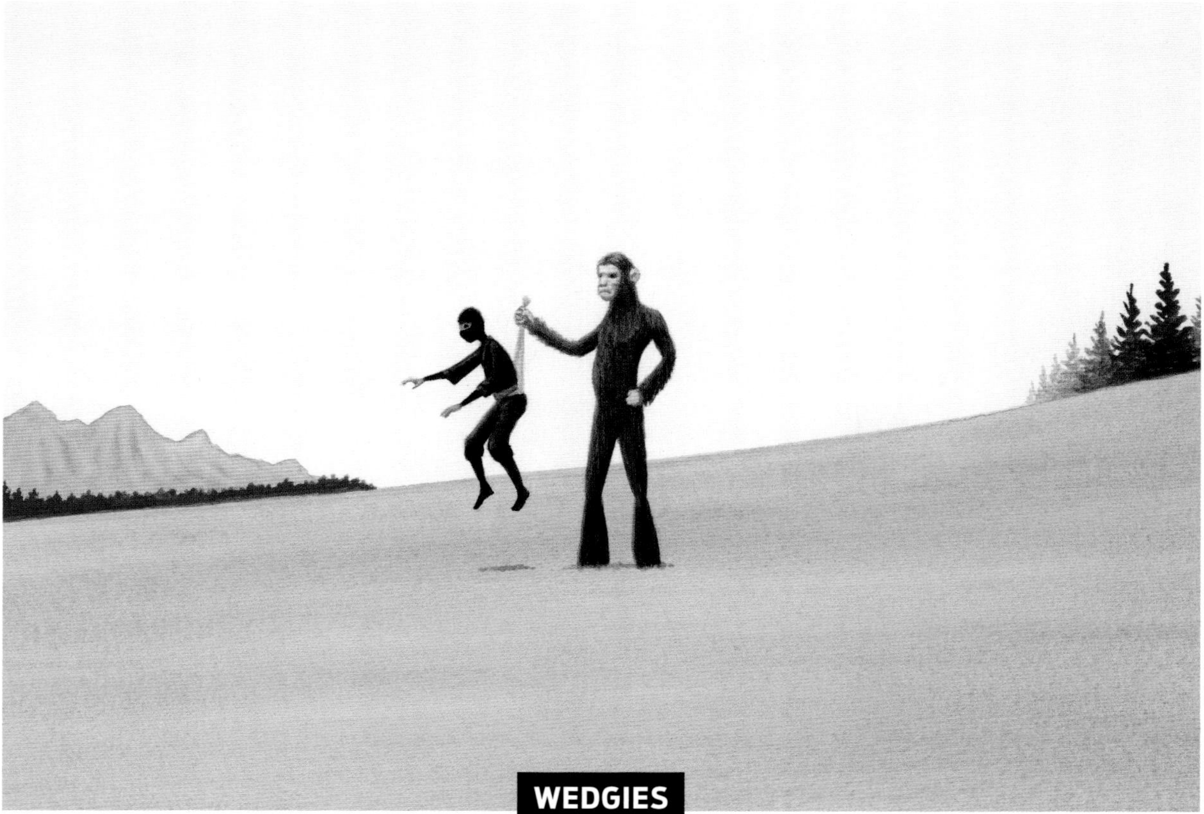

WEDGIES

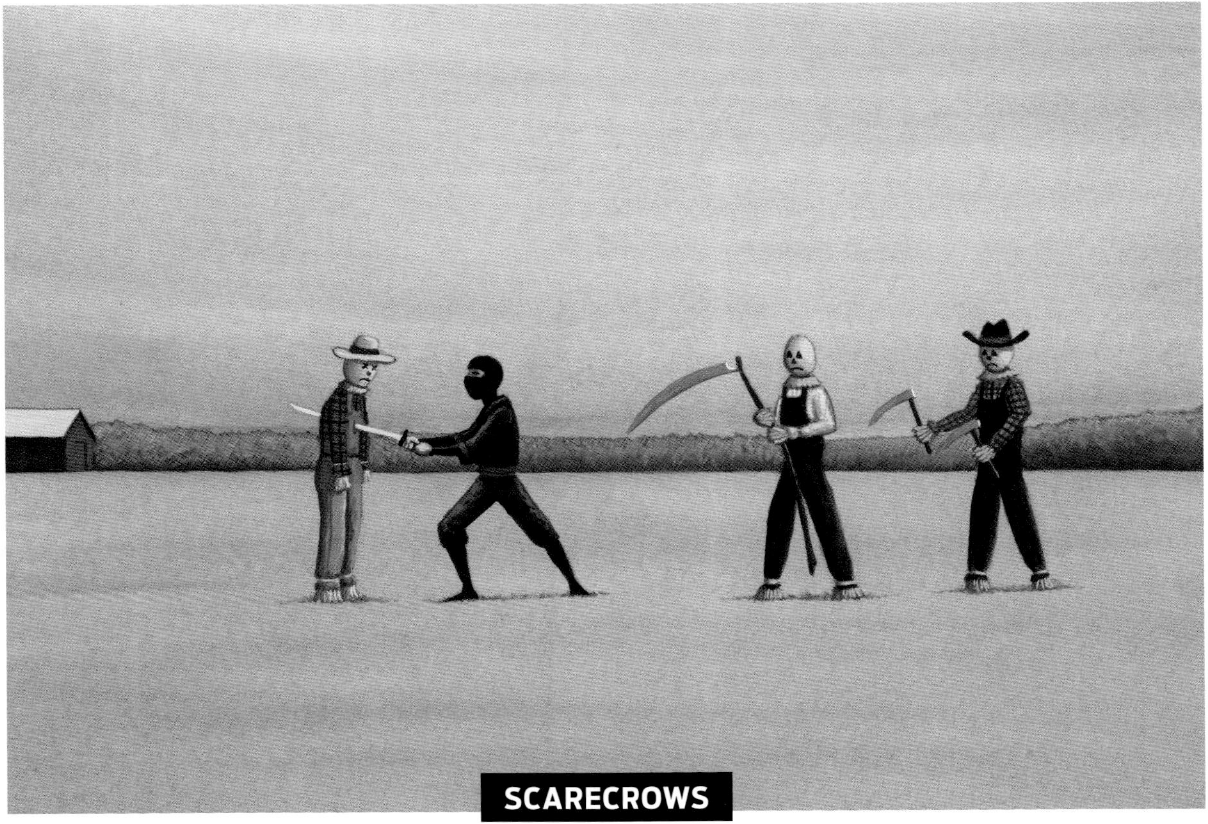

SCARECROWS

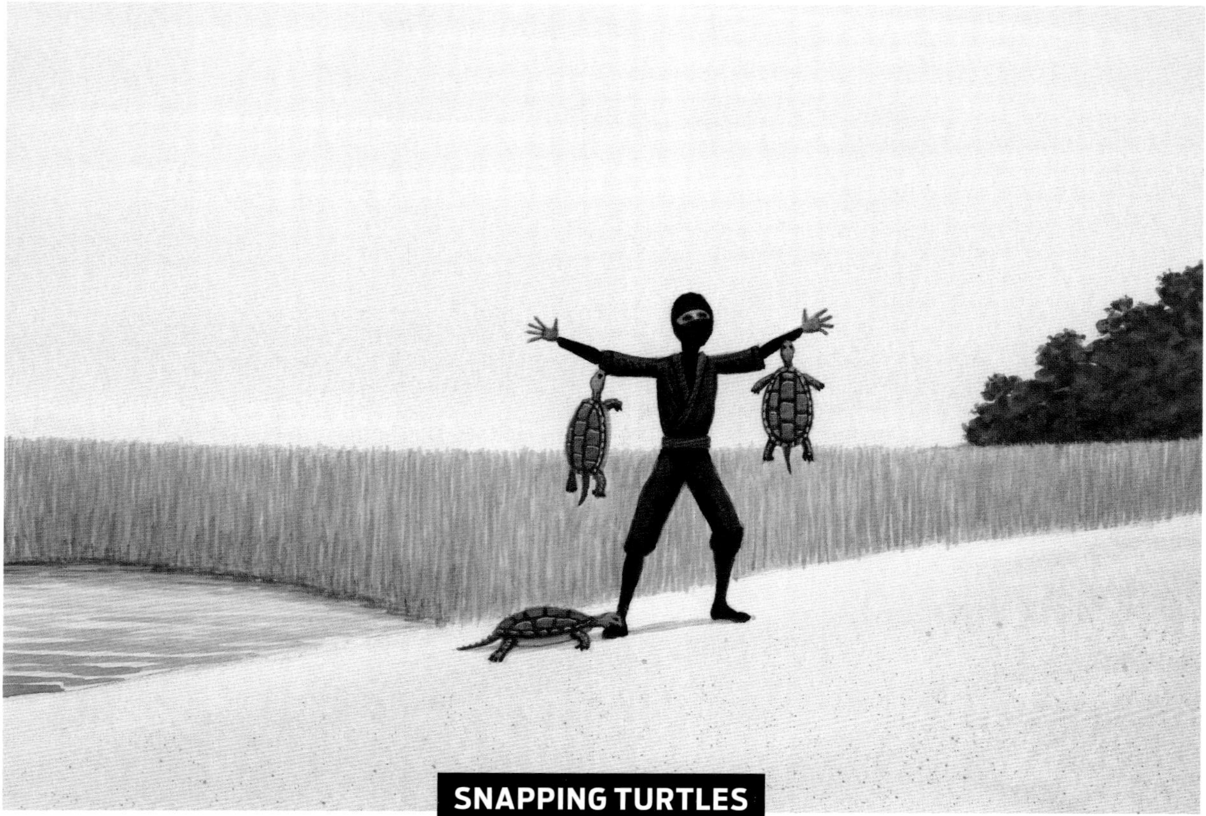

SNAPPING TURTLES

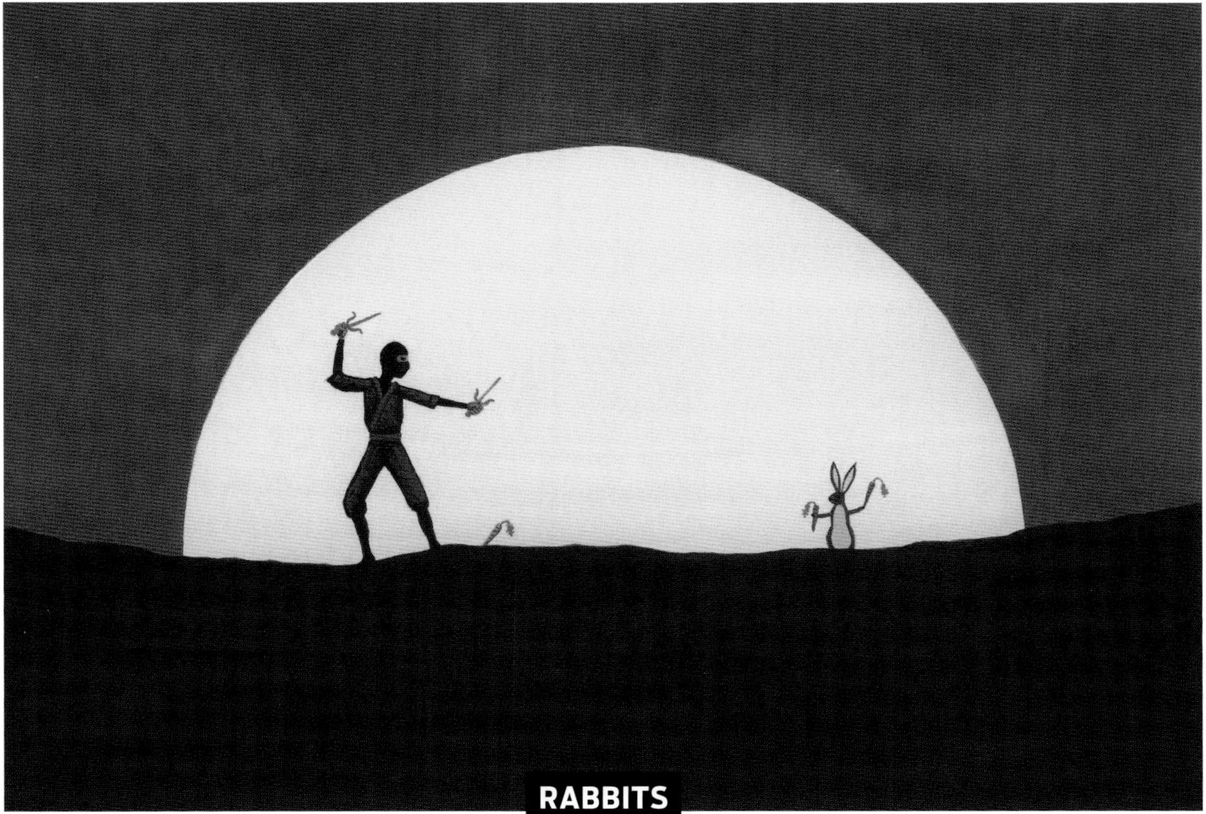

RABBITS

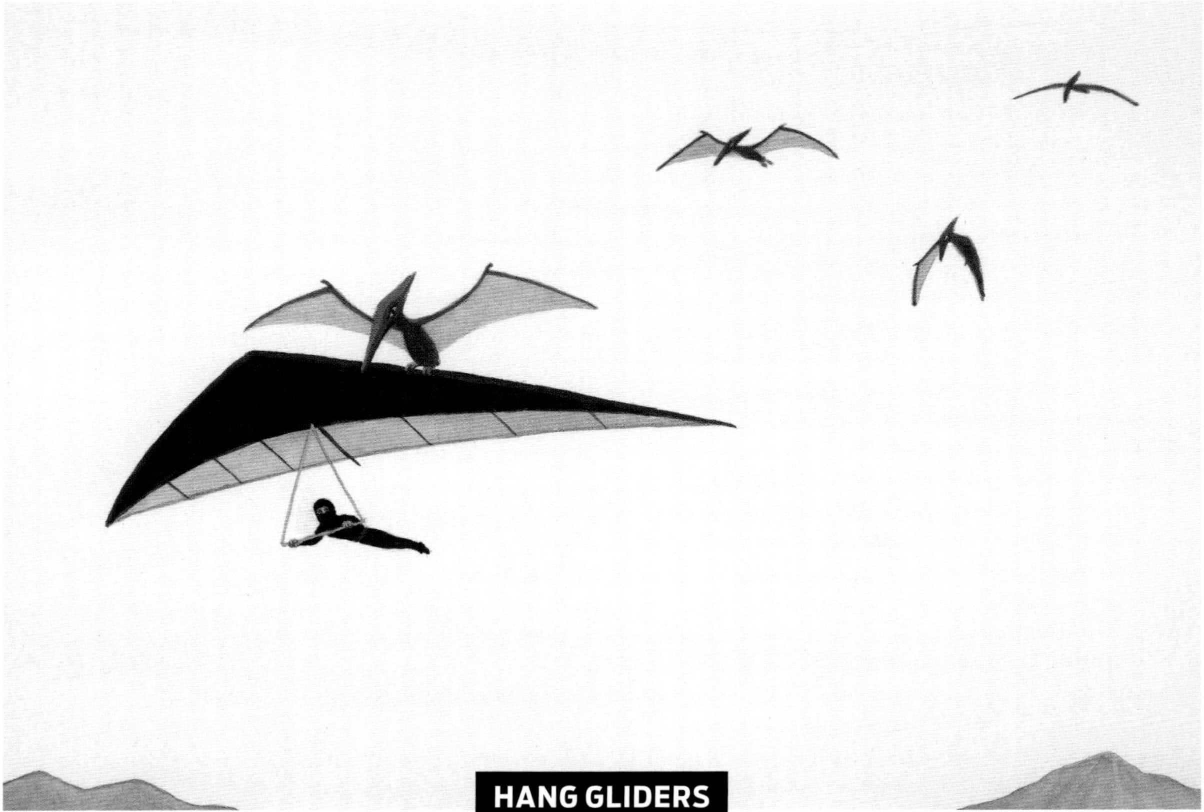

HANG GLIDERS

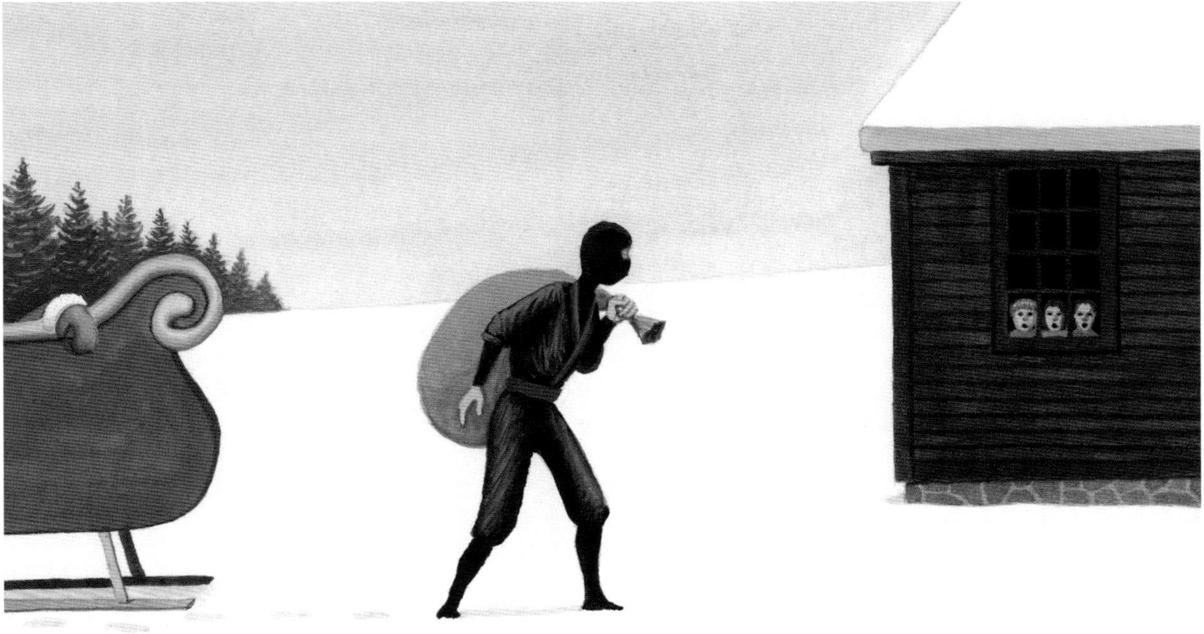

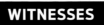

WITNESSES

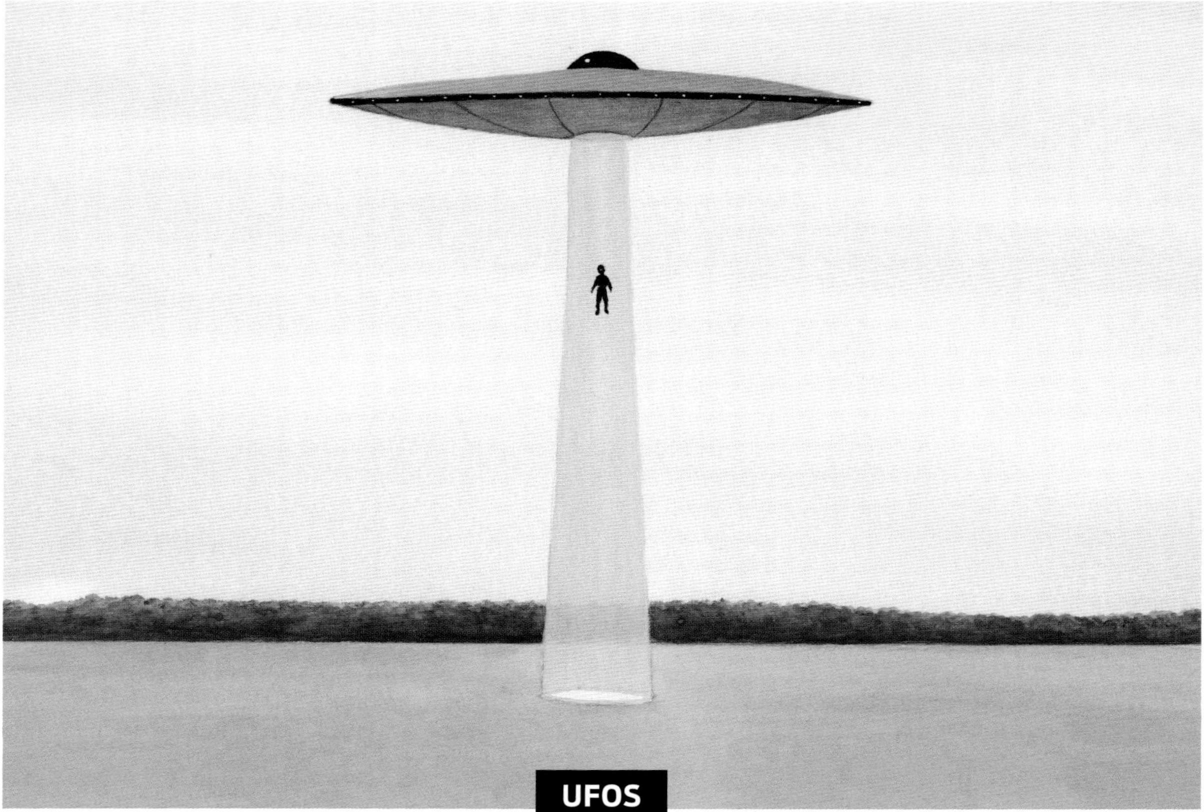

UFOS

NINJAS REALLY ENJOY . . .

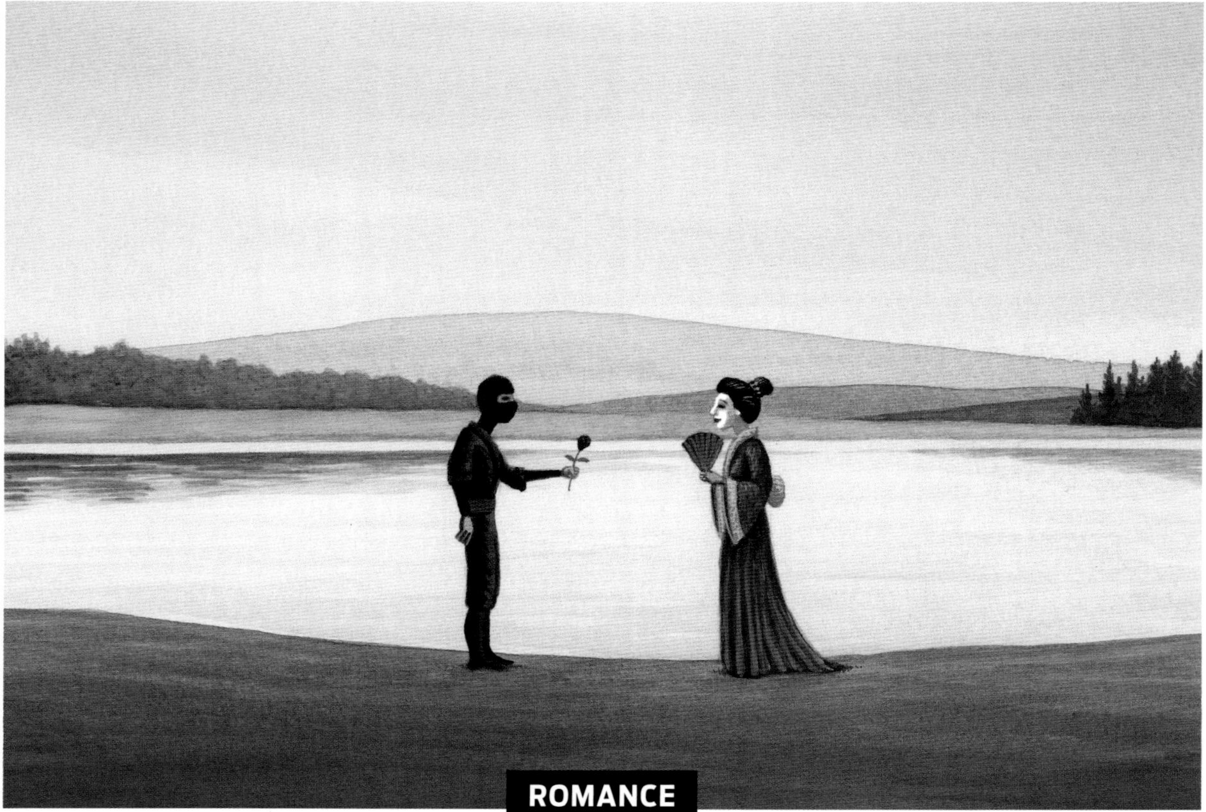

ROMANCE

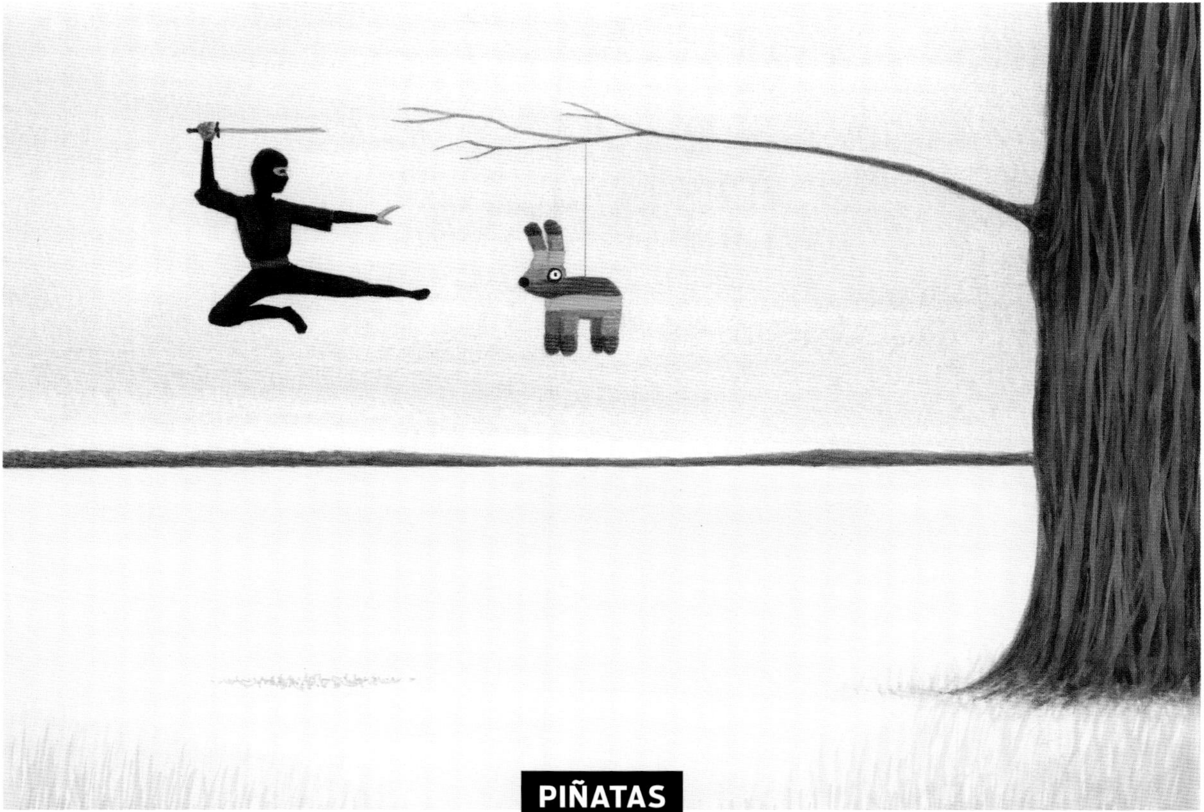

PIÑATAS

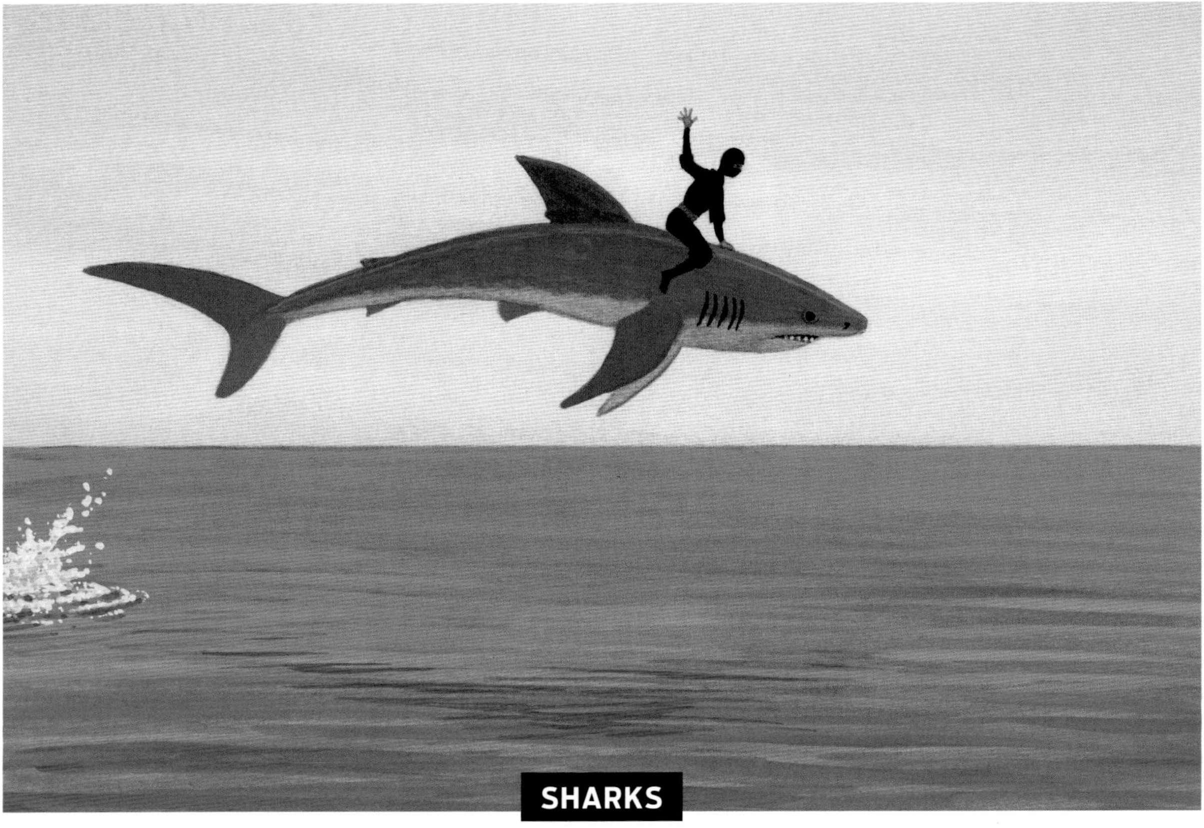

SHARKS

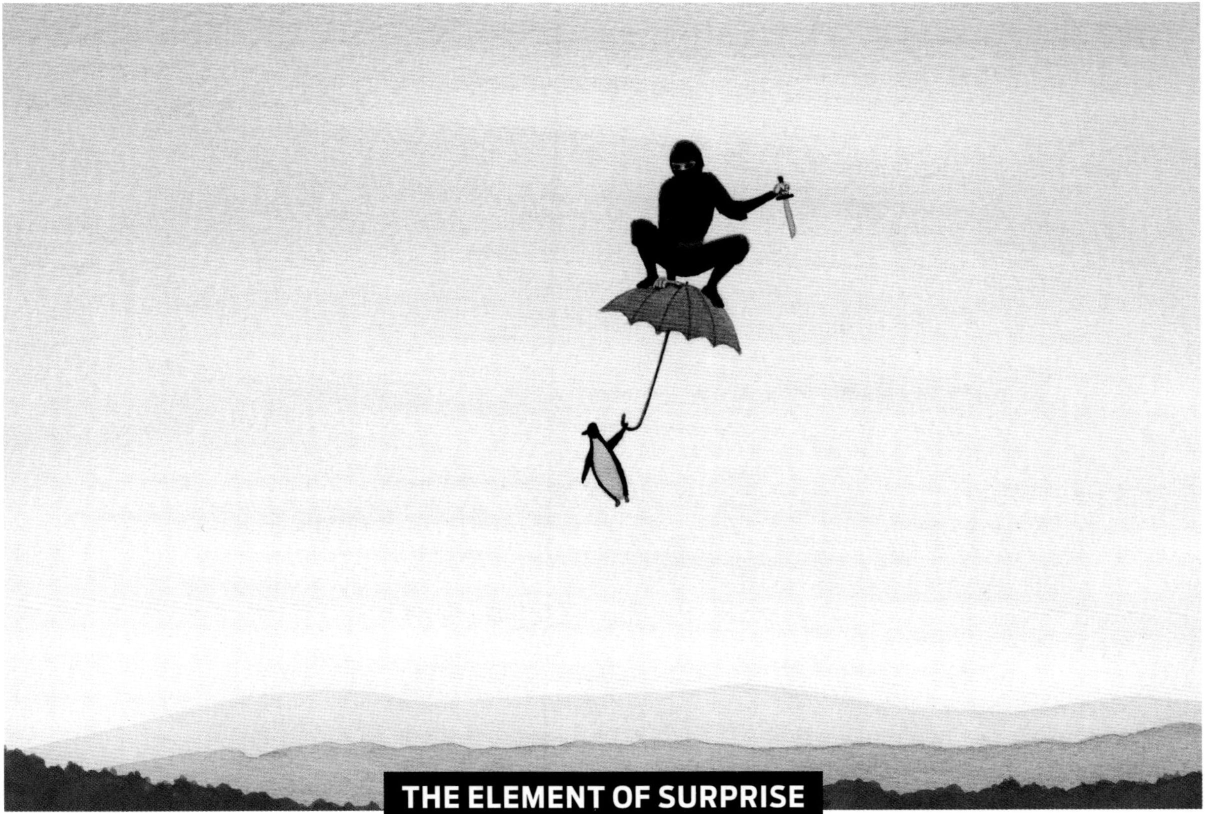

THE ELEMENT OF SURPRISE

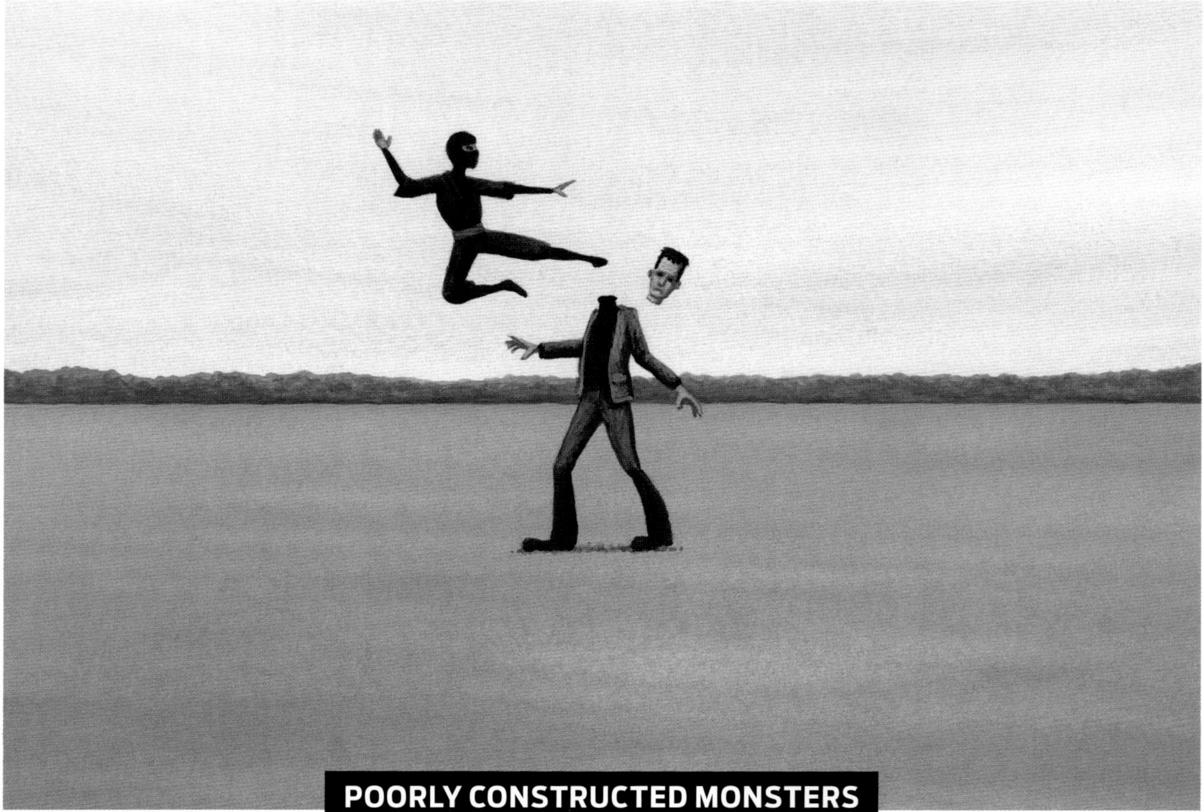

POORLY CONSTRUCTED MONSTERS

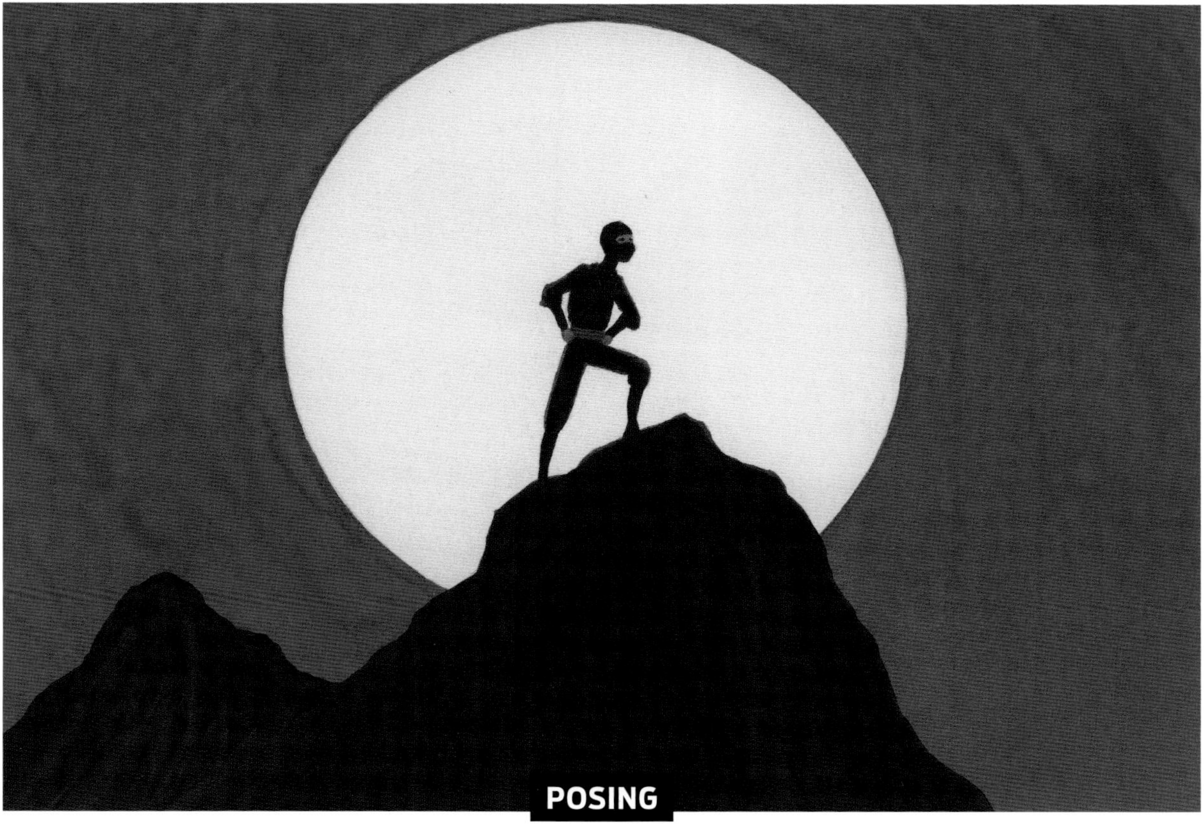

POSING

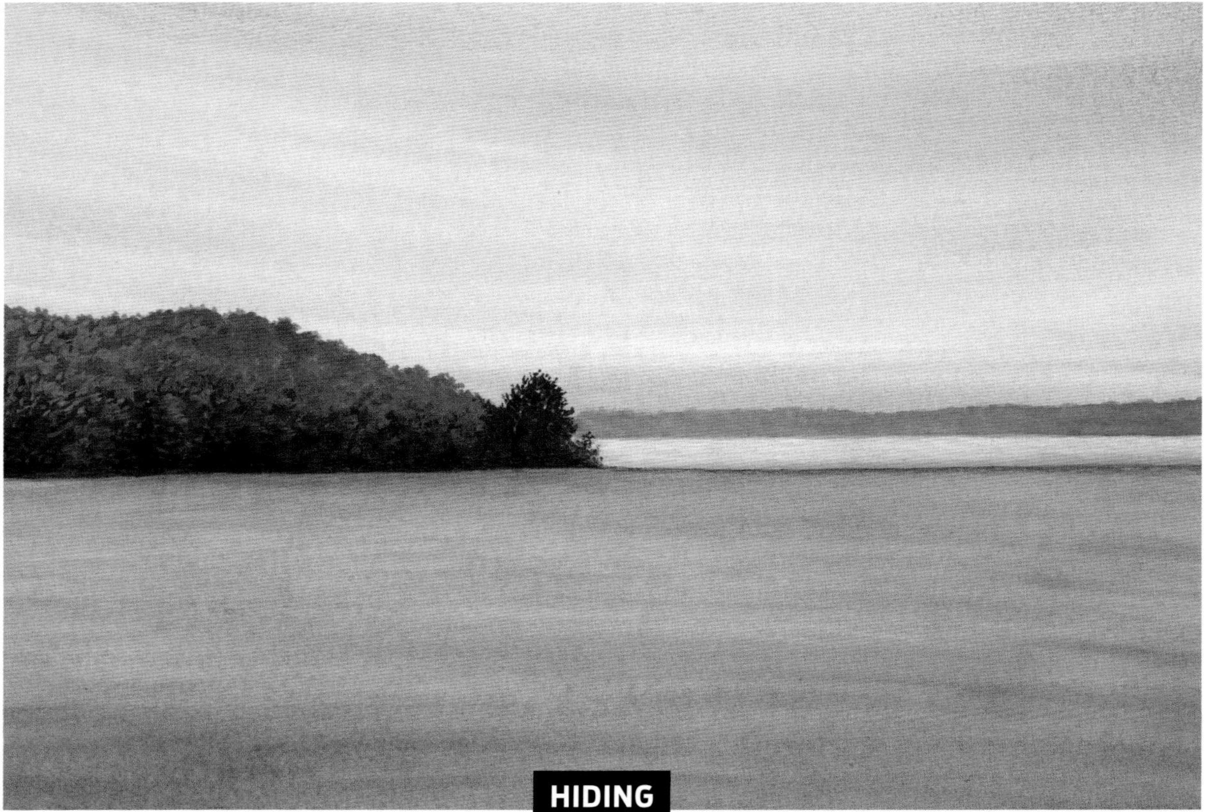

HIDING

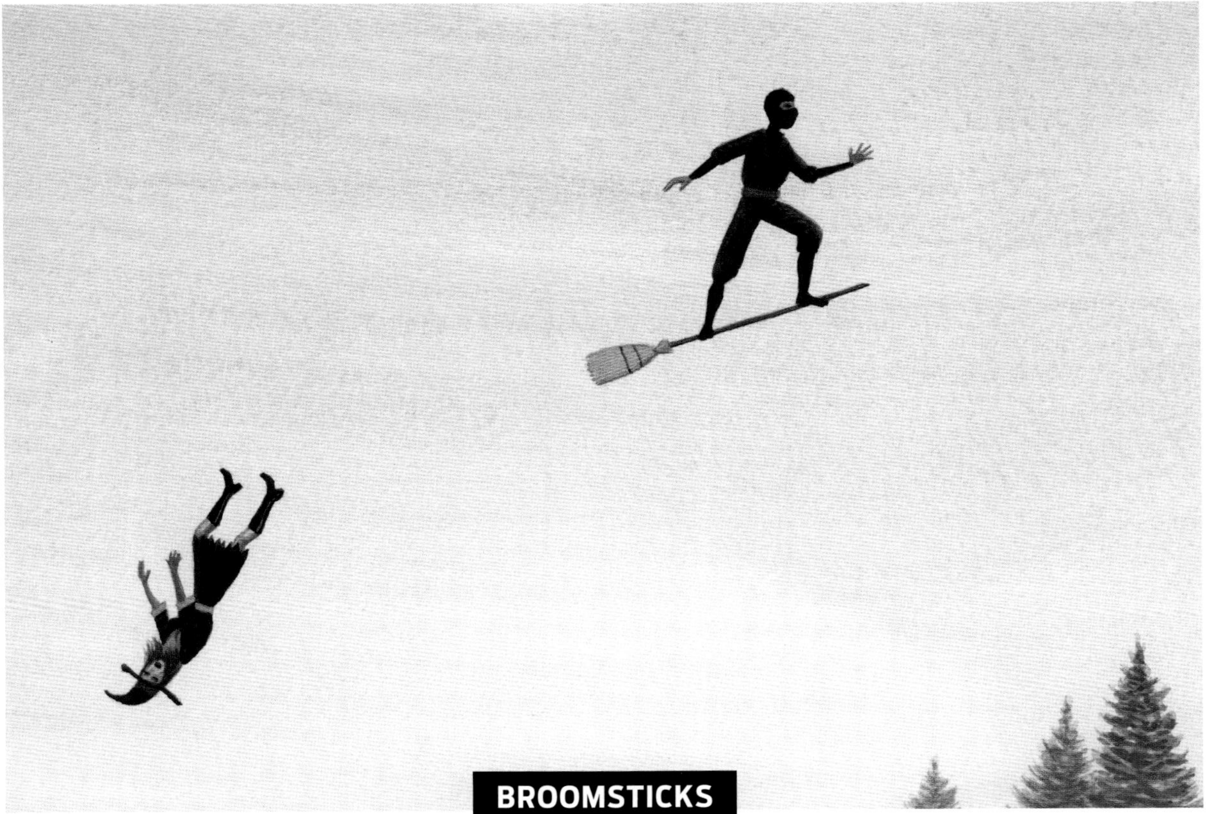

BROOMSTICKS

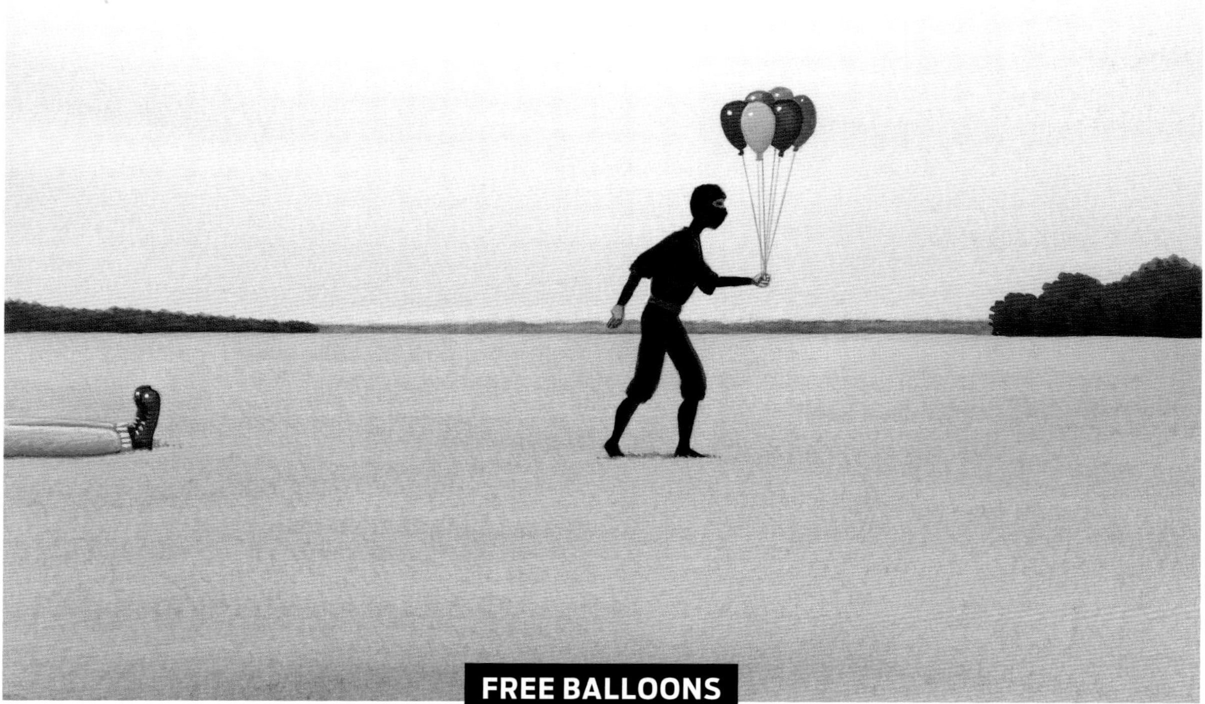

FREE BALLOONS

NINJAS HAVE MAJOR ISSUES WITH . . .

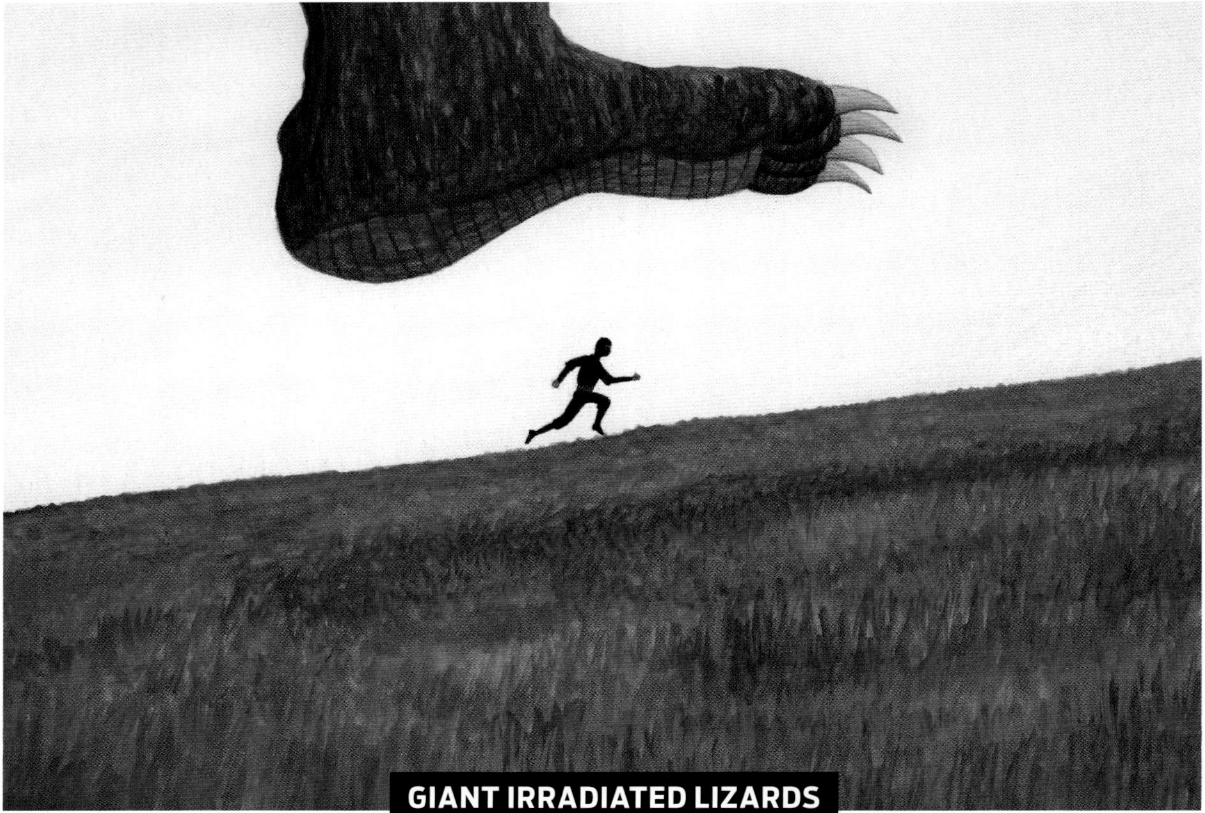

GIANT IRRADIATED LIZARDS

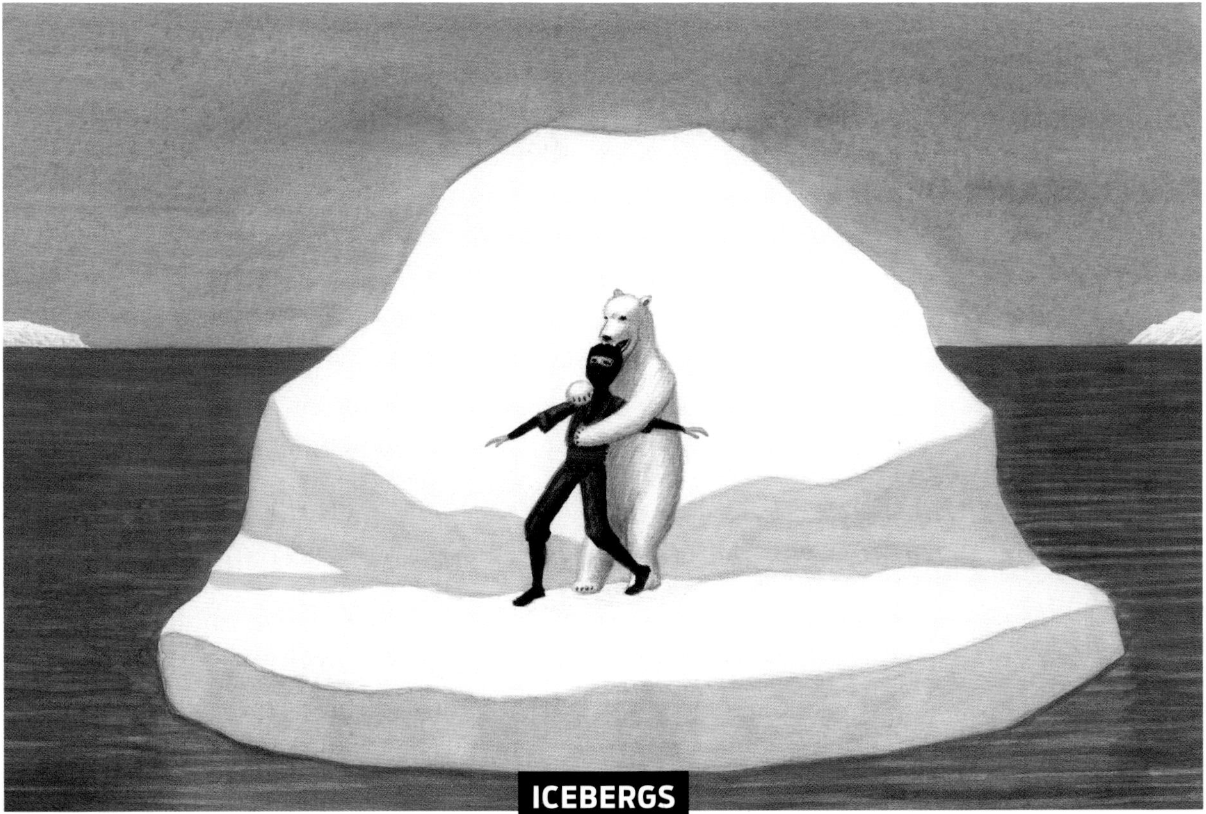

ICEBERGS

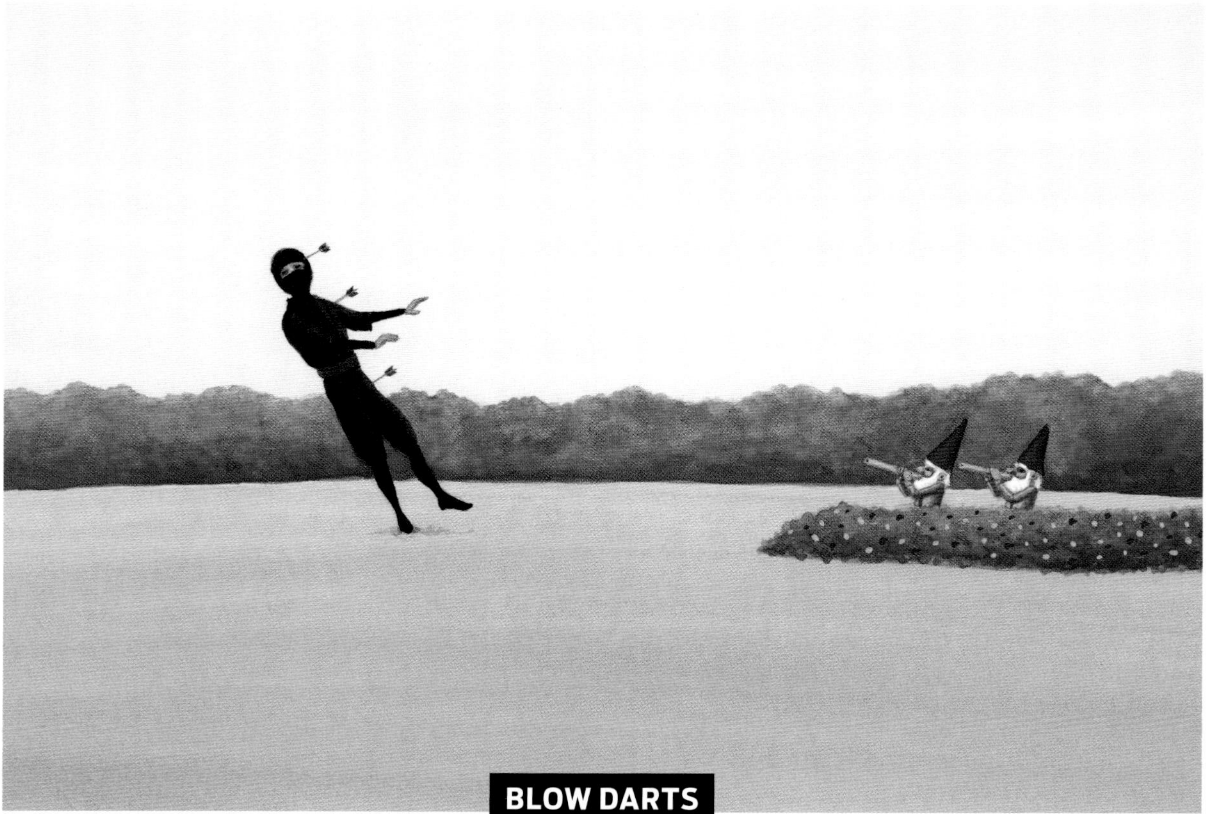
BLOW DARTS

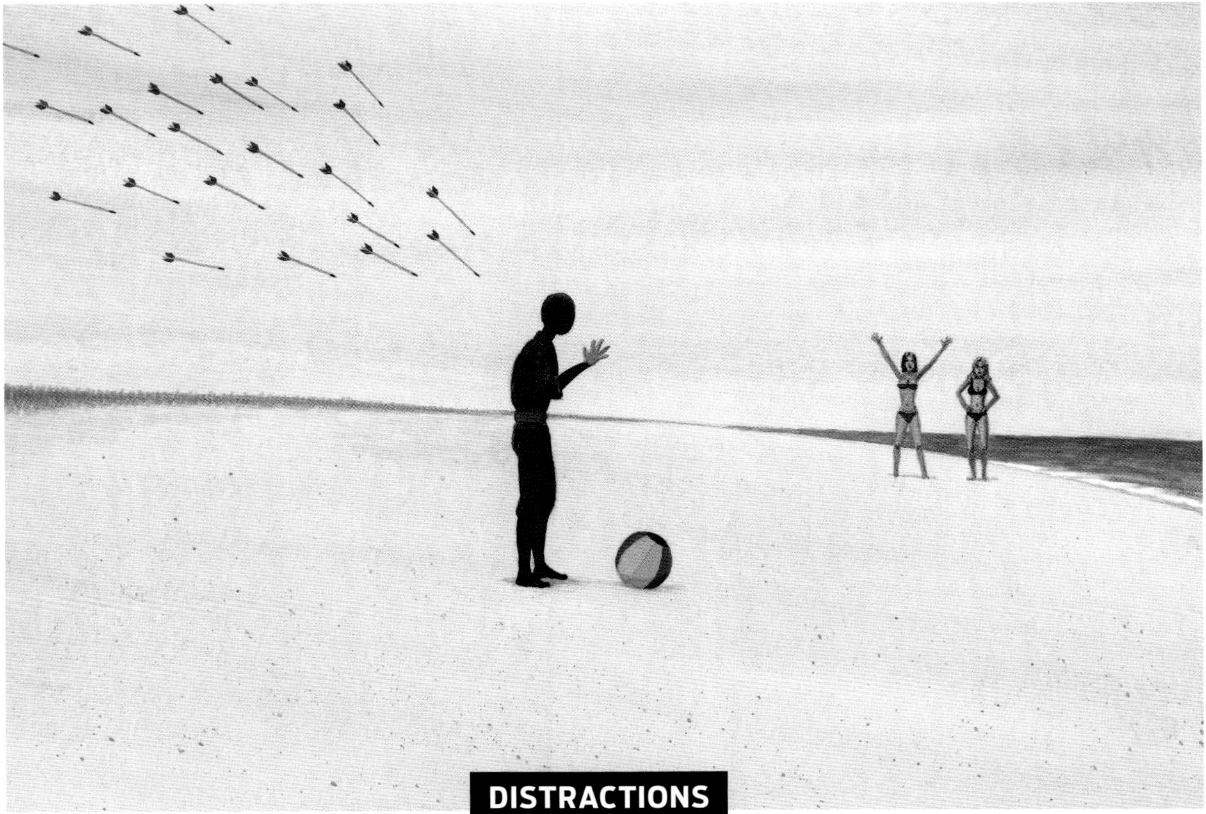

DISTRACTIONS

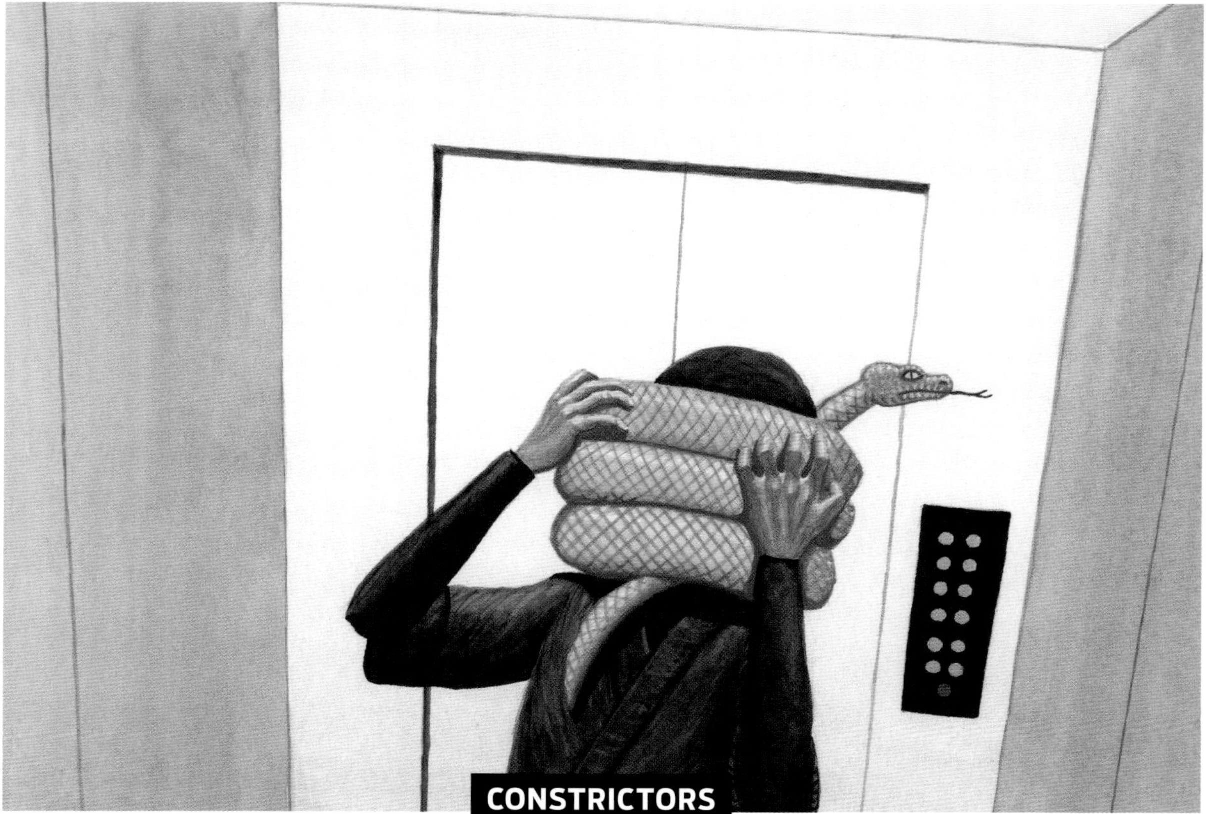

CONSTRICTORS

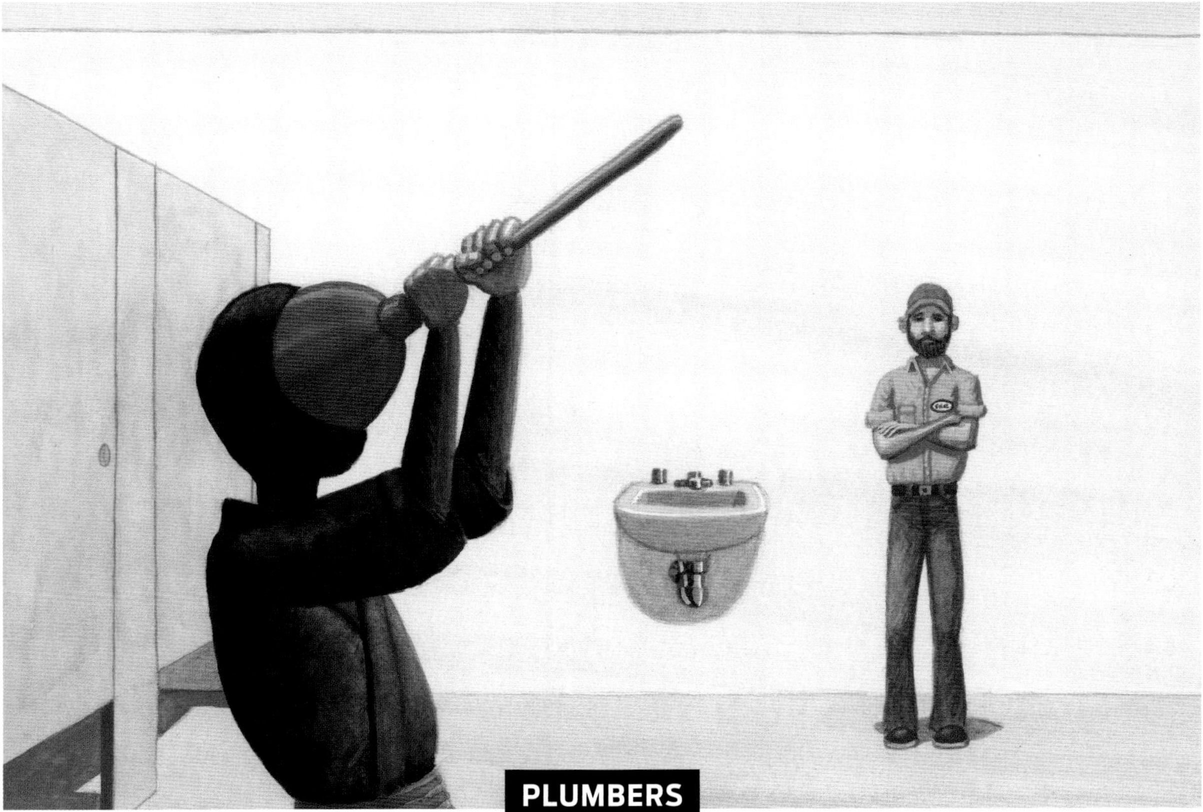

PLUMBERS

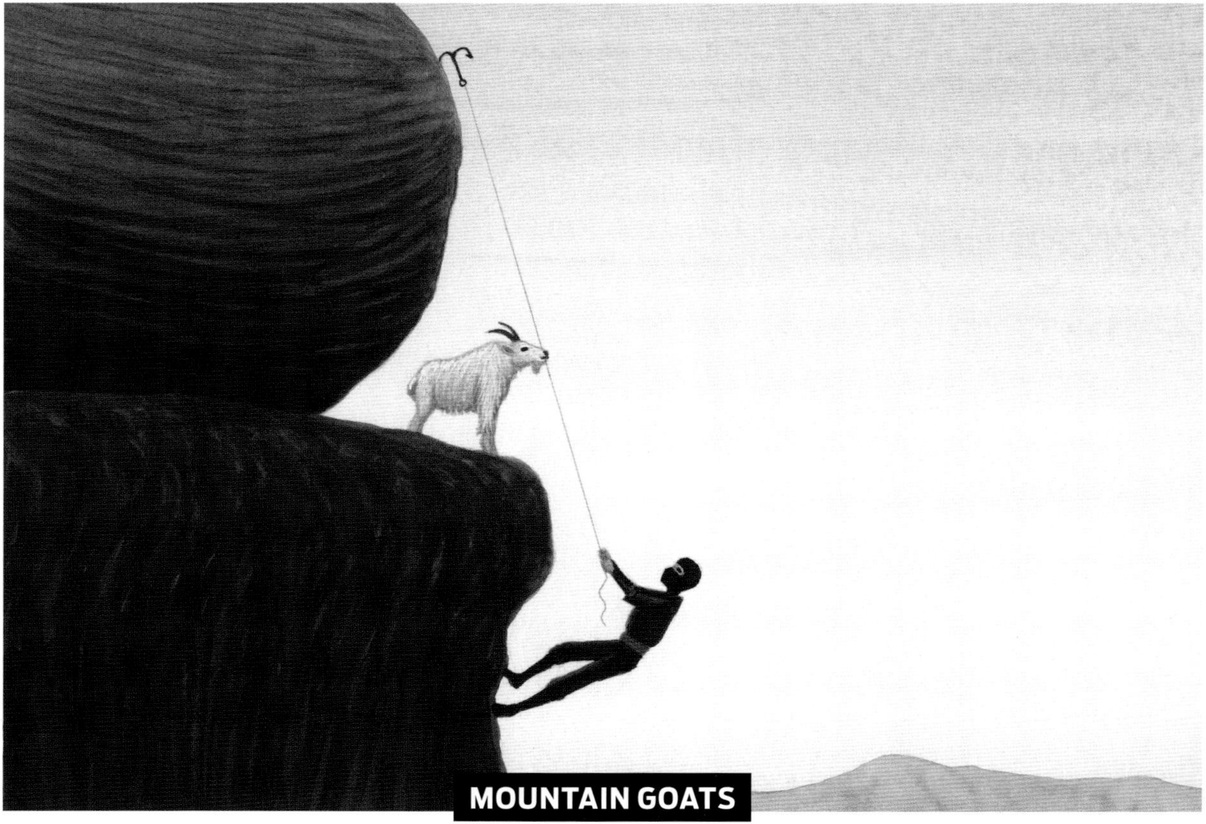

MOUNTAIN GOATS

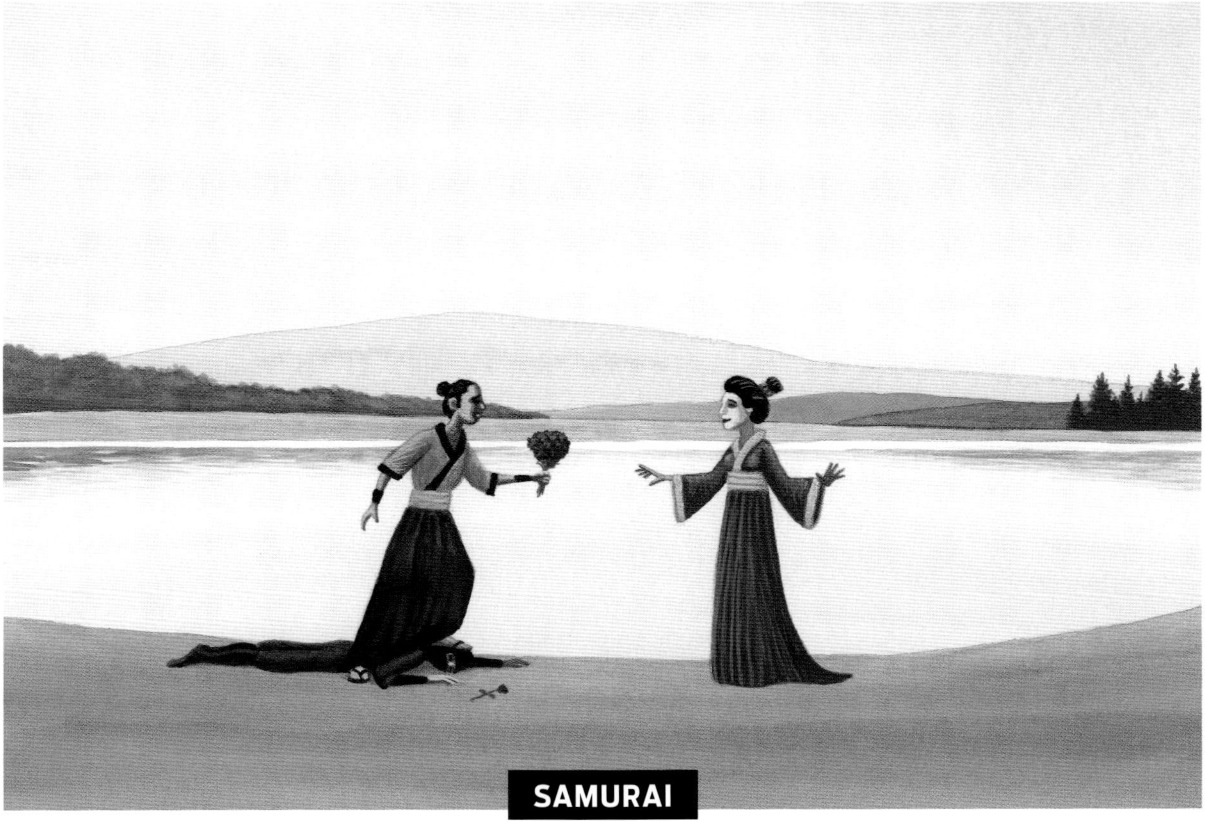

SAMURAI

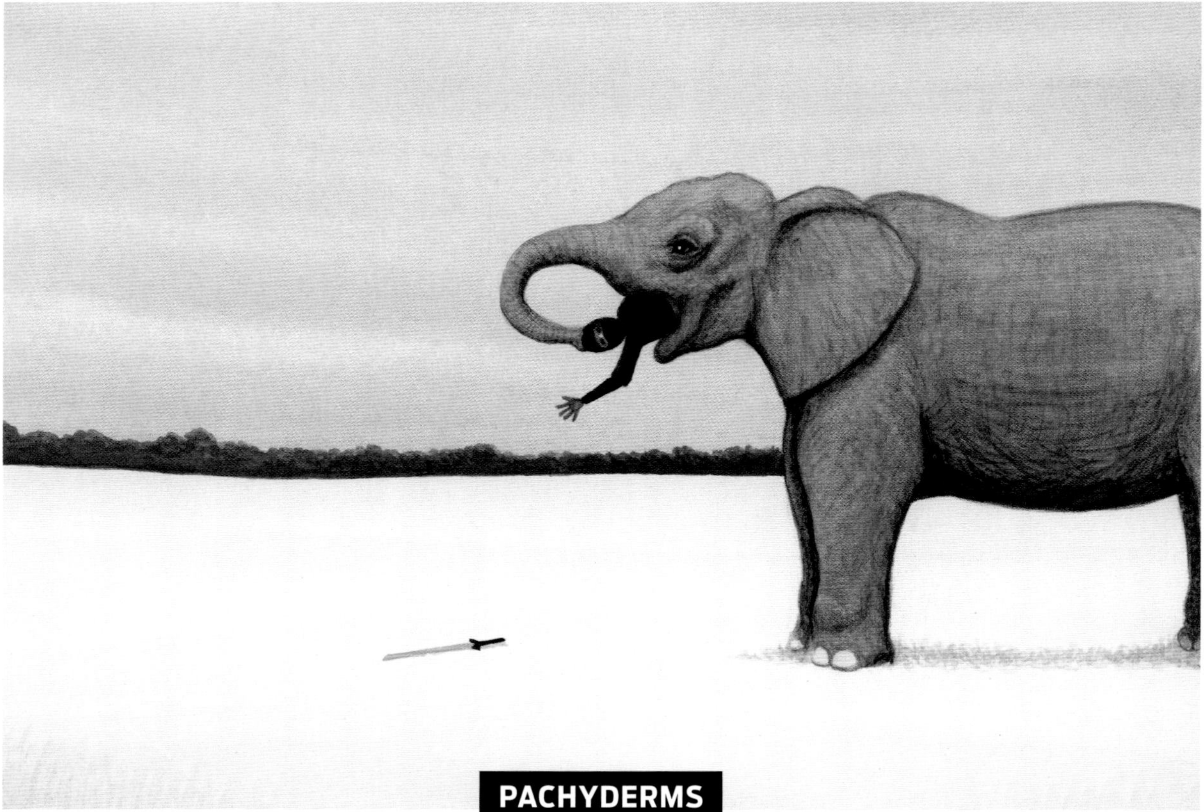

PACHYDERMS

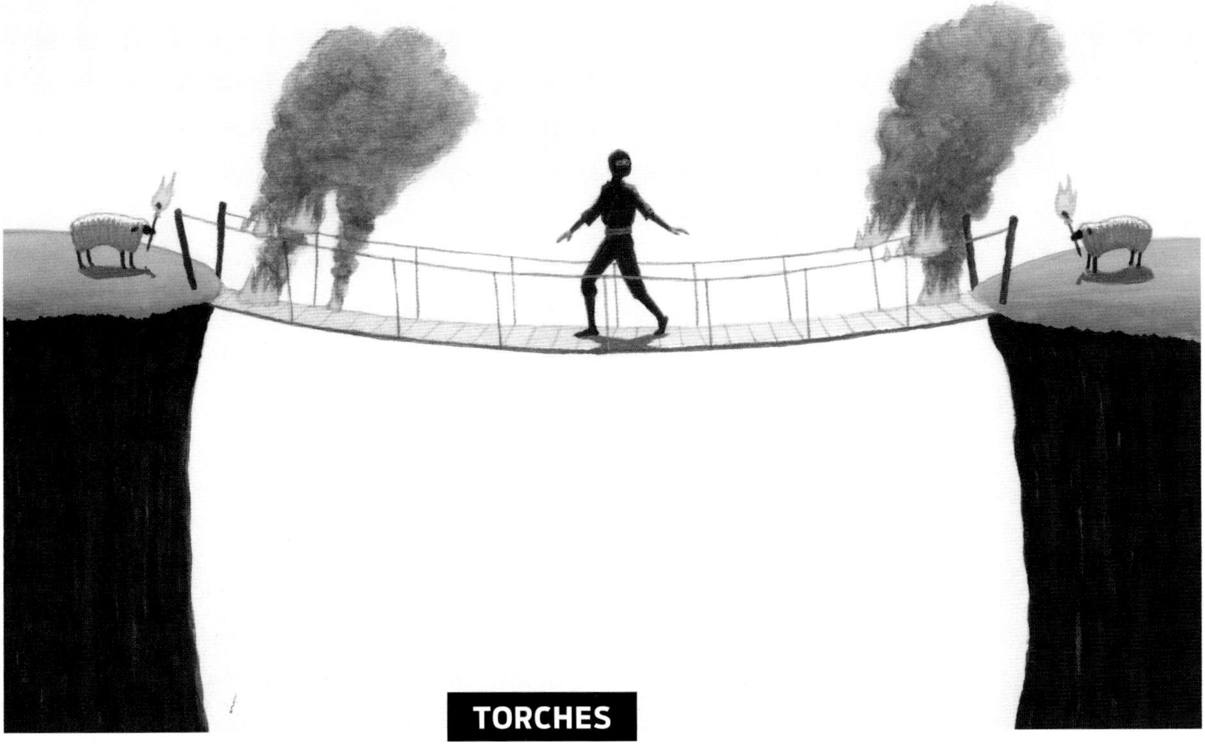

TORCHES

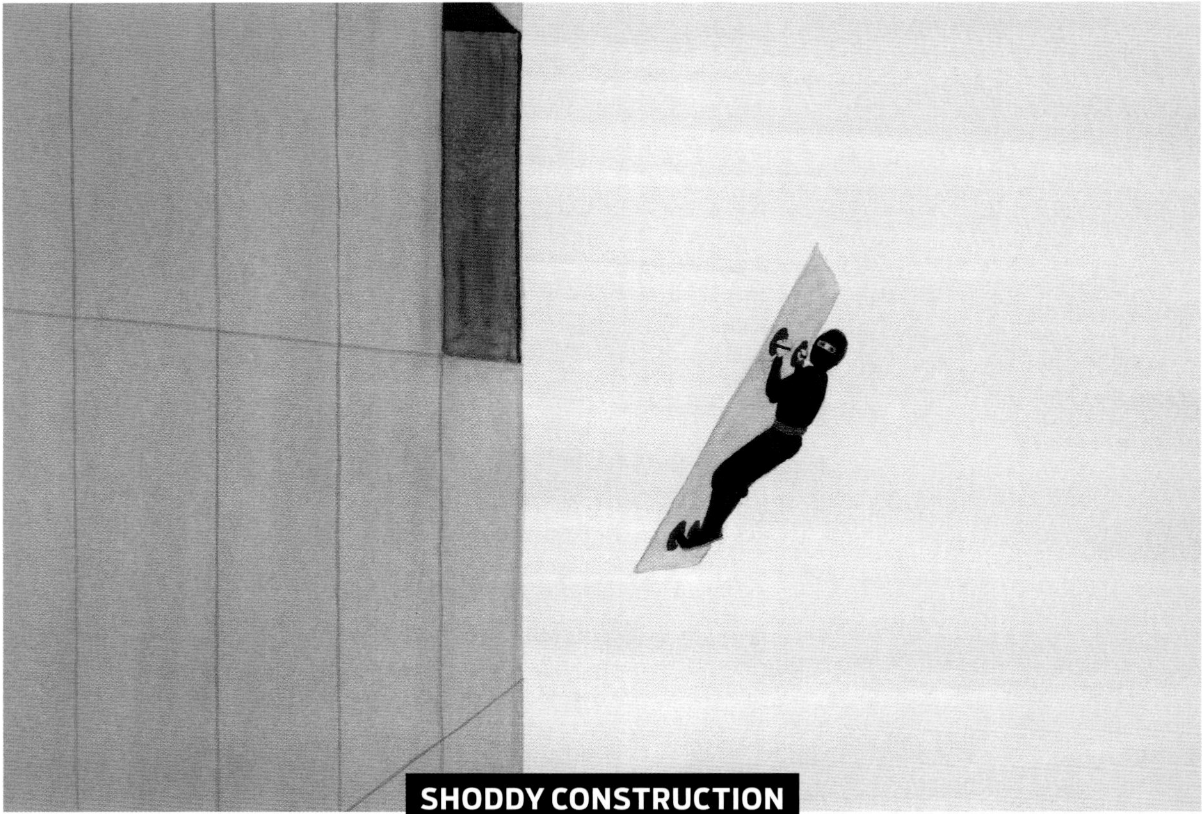

SHODDY CONSTRUCTION

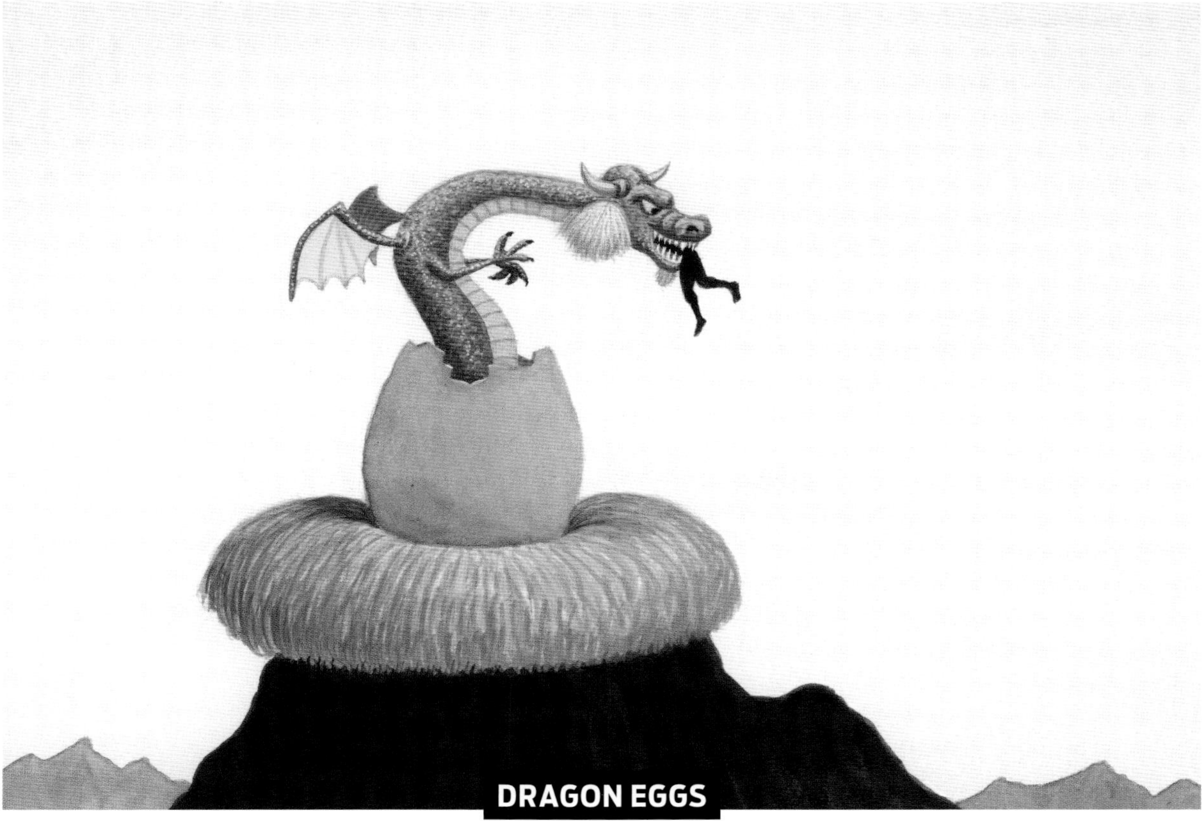

DRAGON EGGS

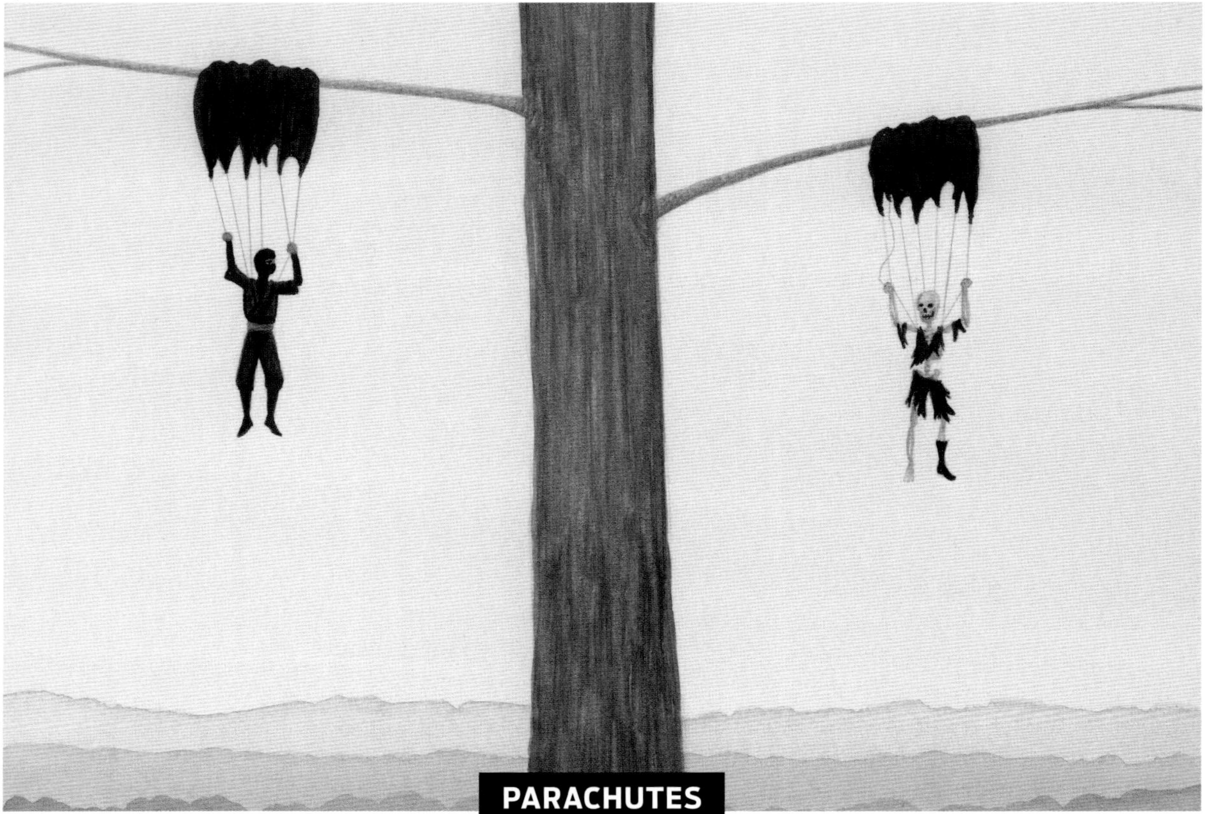

PARACHUTES

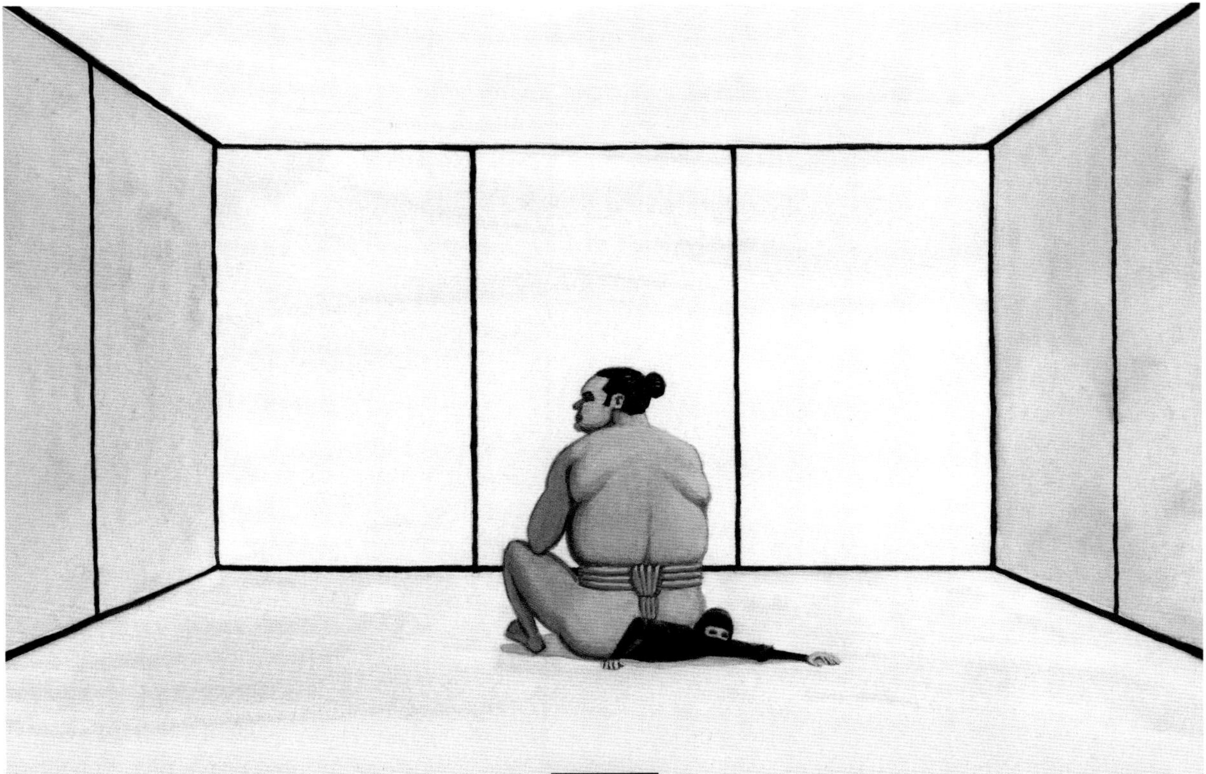

SUMO

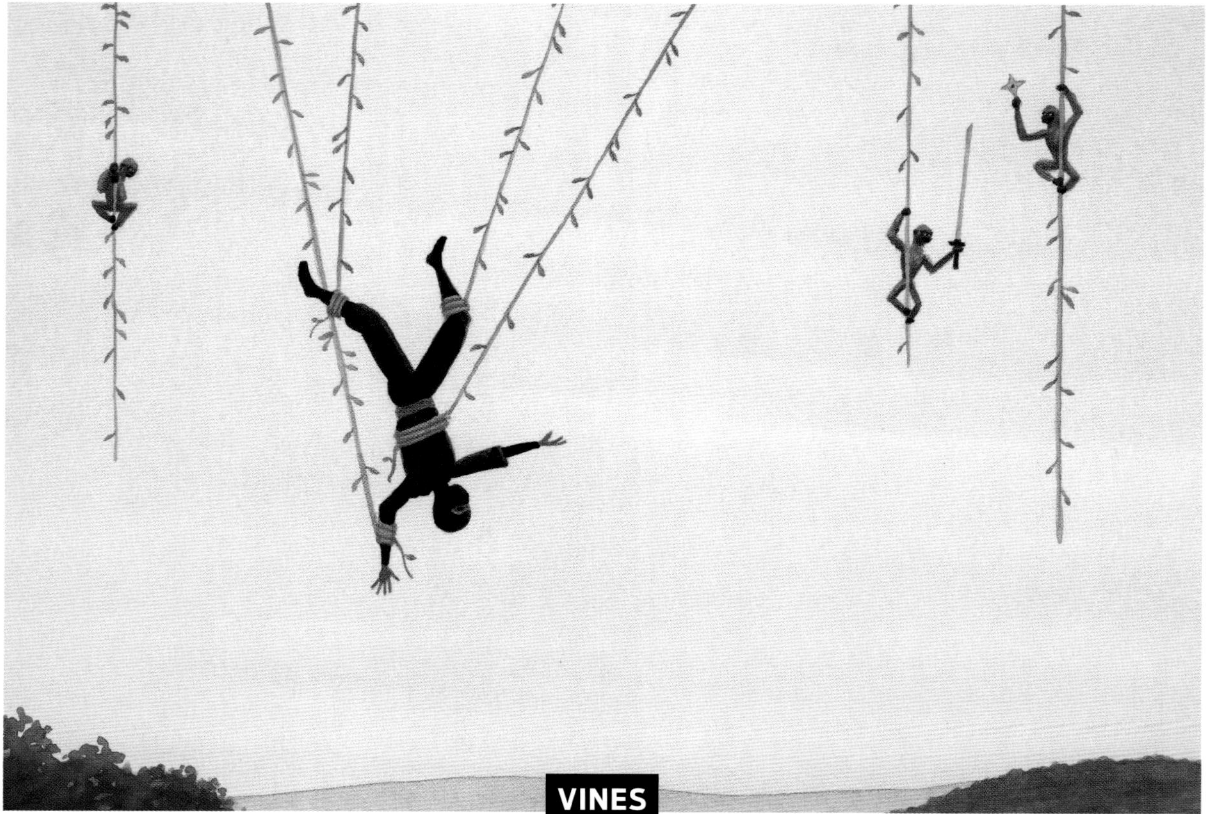

VINES

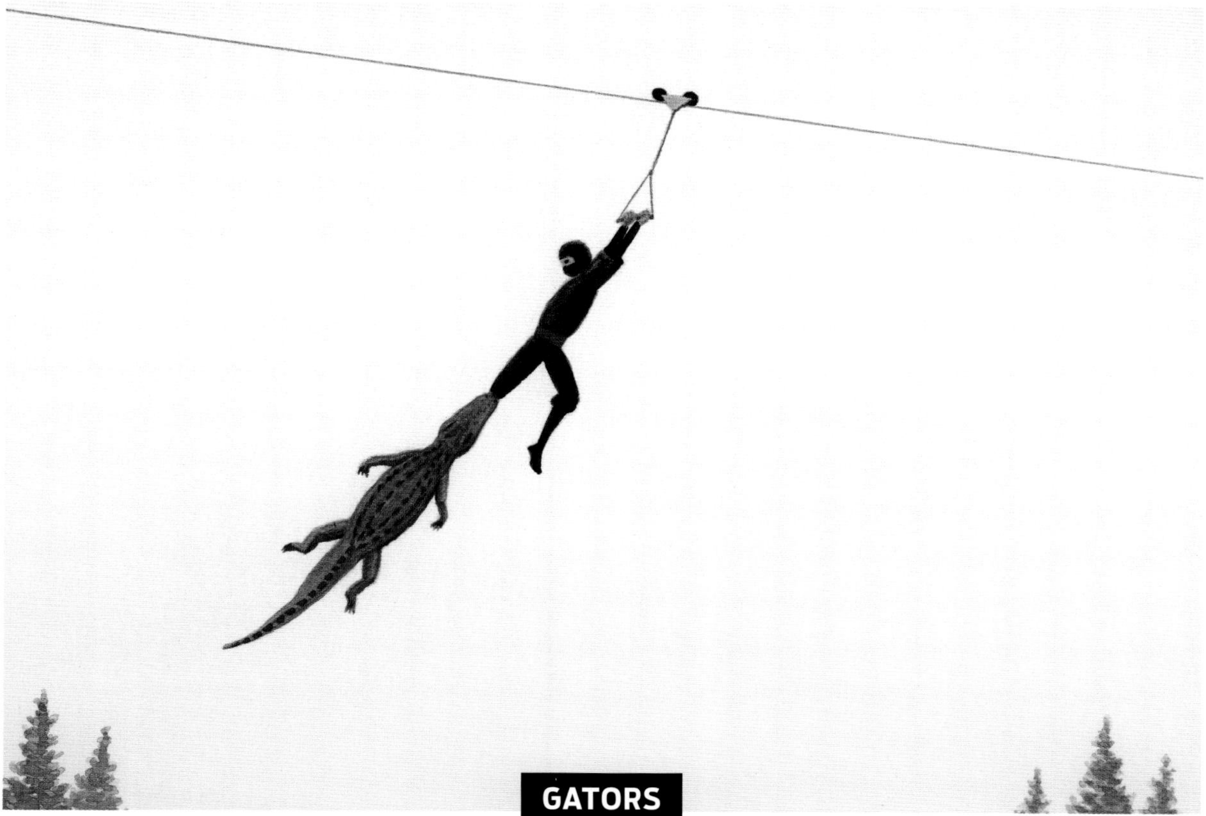

GATORS

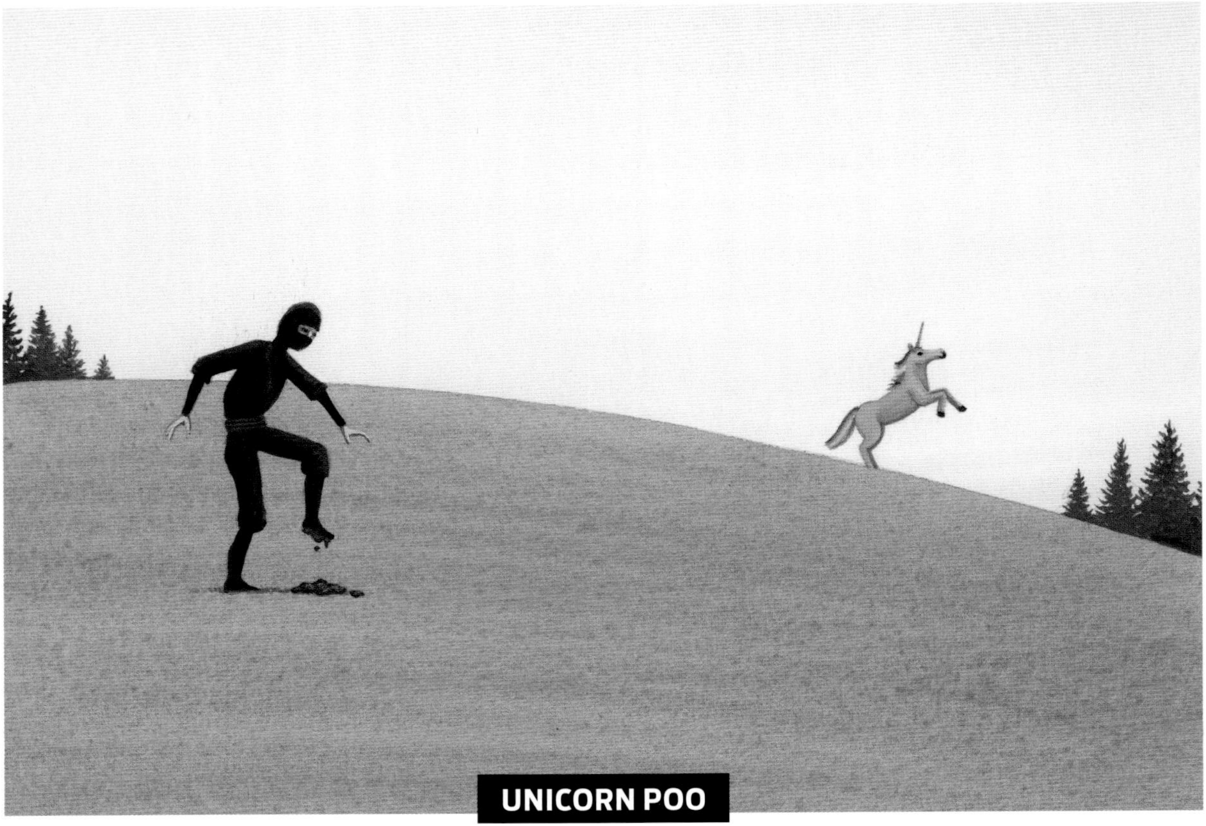

UNICORN POO

NINJAS SECRETLY LONG FOR . . .

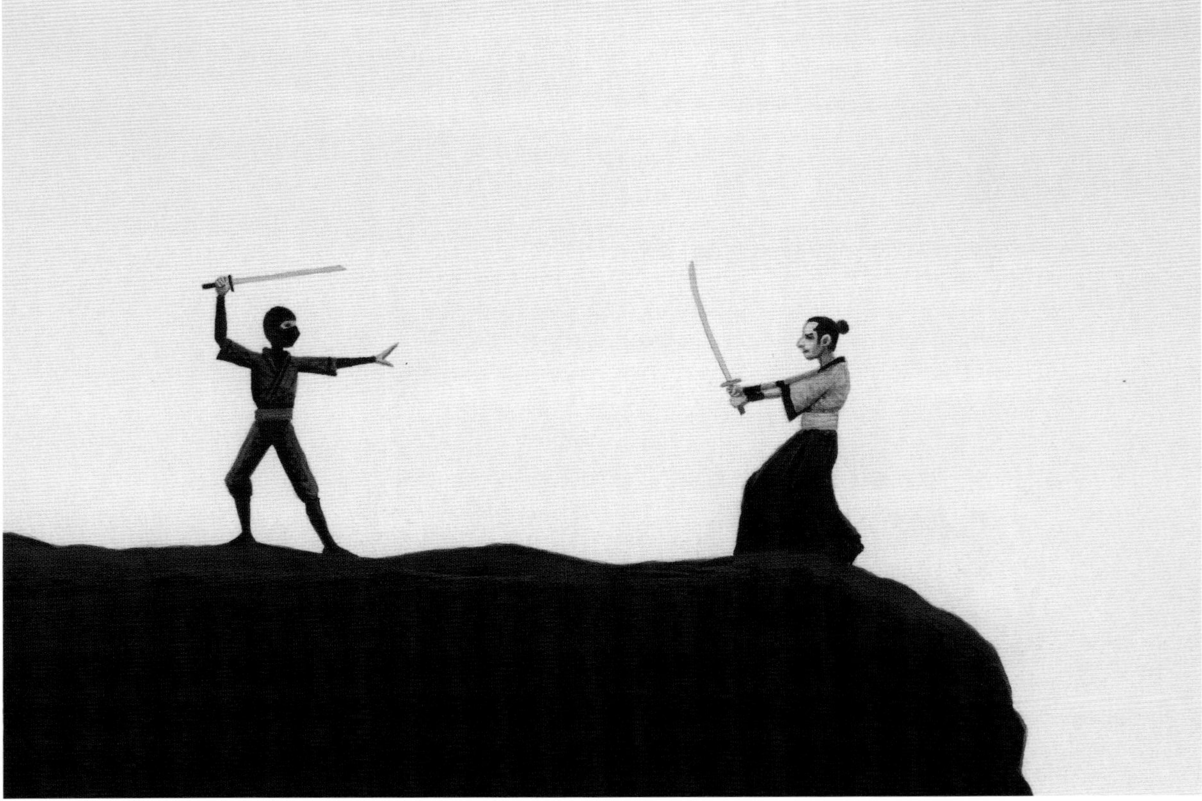

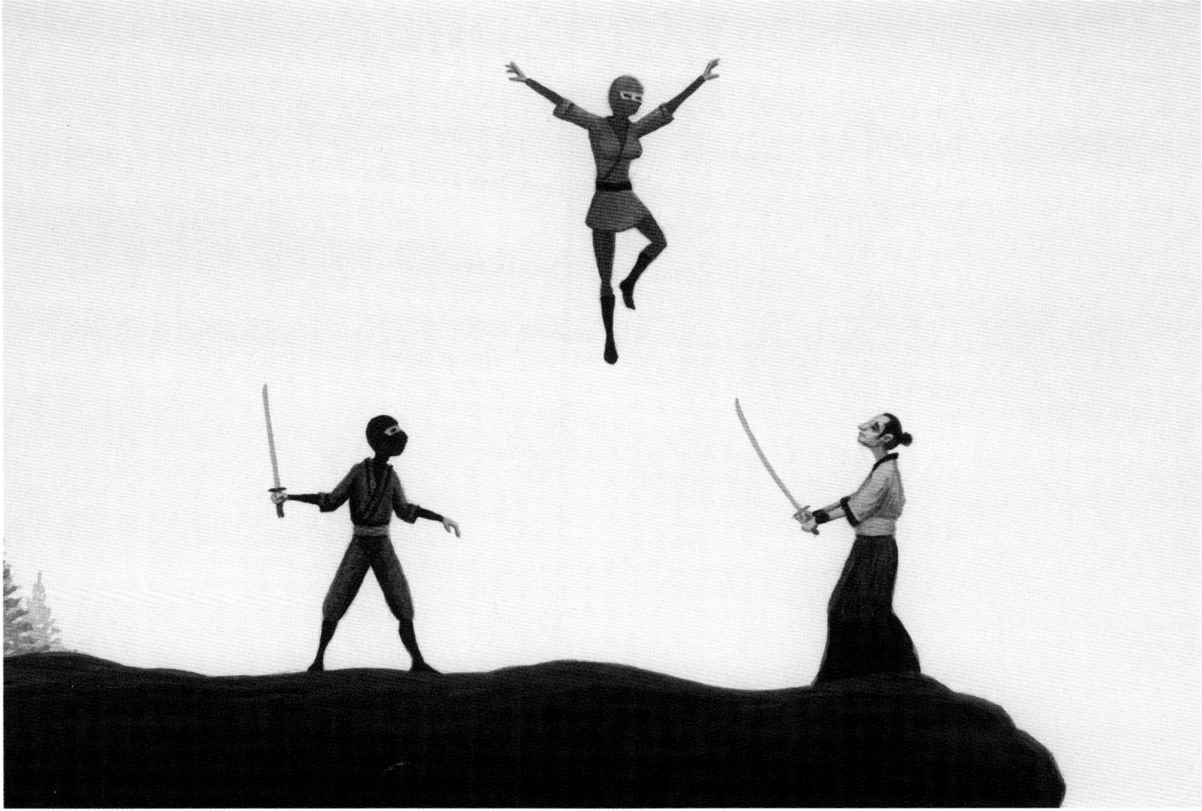

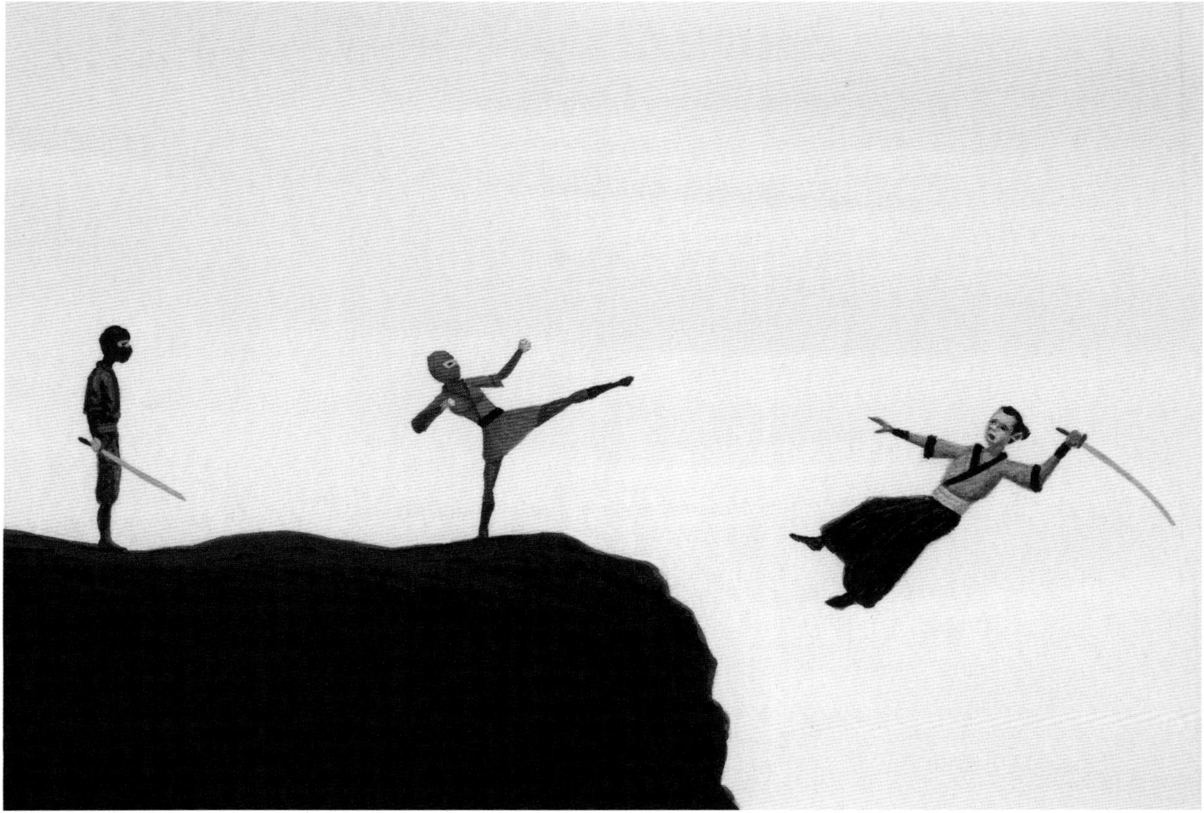

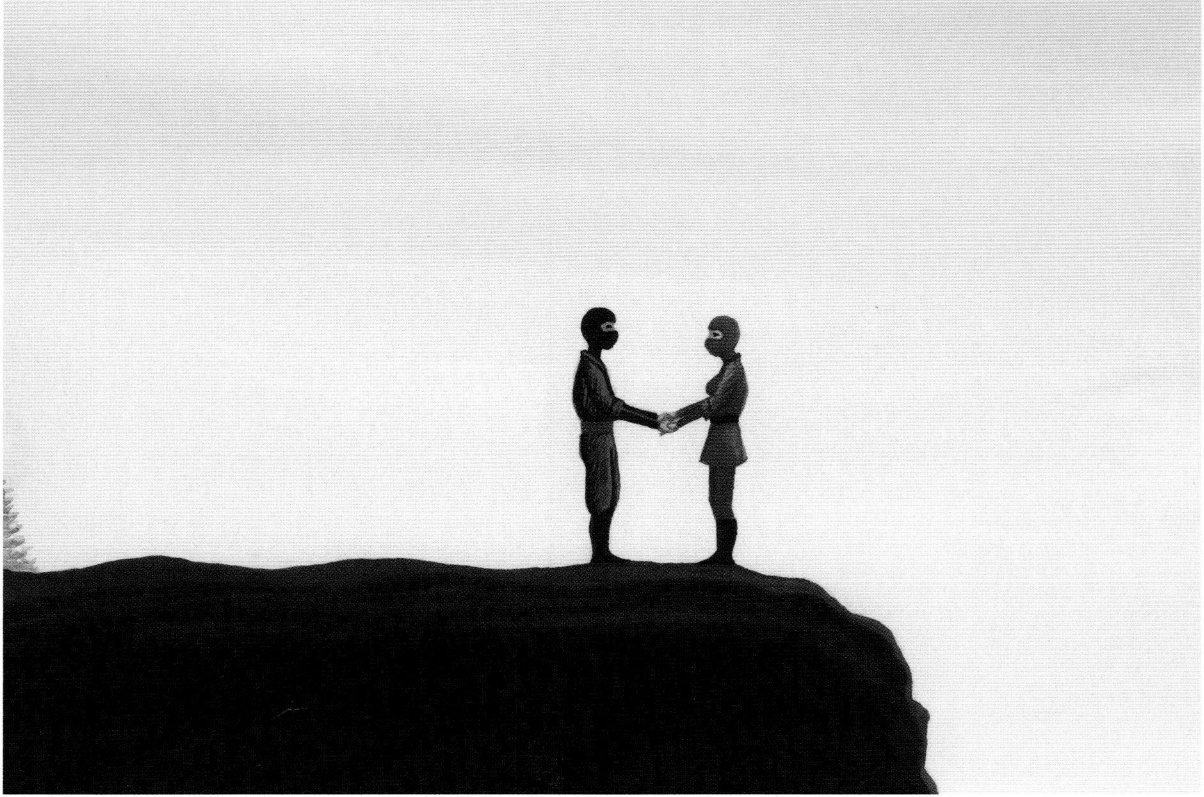

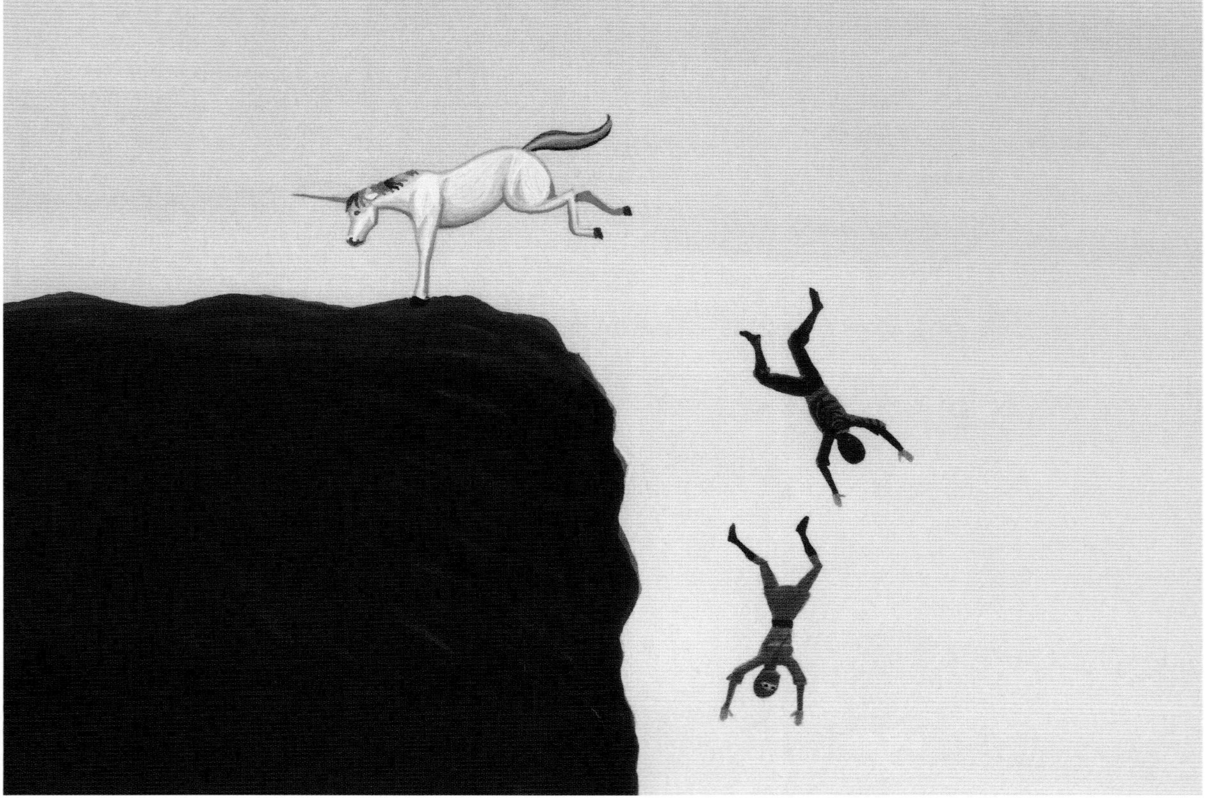